The Story of L33

And How the Zeppelins Were Defeated

Paul Mussett

Copyright © Paul Mussett 2024

All rights reserved.

No part of this publication may be reproduced, distributed, or transmitted in any form or by any means, including photocopying, recording, or other electronic or mechanical methods, without the author's prior written permission, except in the case of brief quotations embodied in critical reviews and certain other non-commercial uses permitted by copyright law. For permission requests, please get in touch with the author.

Contents

Dedication 1

Acknowledgments 2

Introduction 3

    Part 1 6

Chapter 1 7

Chapter 2 16

Chapter 3 27

Chapter 4 39

Chapter 5 43

    Part 2 48

Chapter 1 49

Chapter 2 66

Bibliography 72

Dedication

To my wife Tessa and brother Peter for their support and encouragement.

Acknowledgments

The National Archives, Kew; Mersea Island Museum; The Essex Police Museum; Essex Record Office; The Zeppelin Museum Archive and Library Friedrichshafen.

Introduction

With the titanic battle of the Somme still raging on the Western Front, on a still balmy night in late September 1916, a force of 21 officers and men from the Imperial German Navy were marching through the lanes of rural Essex. However, they were not part of an invasion force so long feared by the residents of the east coast of England, but the crew of the German Navy Zeppelin L33, which on her first operational mission had force-landed in the tiny Essex hamlet of Little Wigborough. The crew were no doubt relieved to be still alive after the determined efforts of both London's anti-aircraft batteries and a single fighter aircraft to bring about their destruction. They were not to enjoy their freedom for long. The crash of the giant airship and the resulting fire attracted the attention of two patrolling special constables, and the crew was soon apprehended. In most cases, they were to spend the rest of the war in prisoner-of-war camps.

Despite the conflagration, the L33 was largely intact. Over the next few days, the aluminium skeleton became a source of great interest, drawing huge crowds of sightseers fascinated by the now-slain monster of the skies. Despite being guarded by troops, numerous "souvenirs" were liberated by locals, much to the irritation of the authorities. Even today, one can occasionally find for sale on eBay items purportedly made out of parts of the airship. Before the wreckage was removed, scientists and engineers had meticulously measured, photographed, and analysed every conceivable aspect of the largely intact carcass. The knowledge gained not only helped to refine anti-Zeppelin measures but also greatly influenced British airship design. It was widely recognised that German airship technology was well in advance of Britain's, so the fortuitous arrival of the latest design provided an impetus to those who hoped to match Germany's achievements in lighter-than-air transportation. Britain's response was the successful post-war R33 airship, which was virtually a copy of the L33.

After the scientists and engineers had completed their tasks, the wreckage was broken up and taken away; the bulk of it ultimately melted down and turned into the Spitfires and Hurricanes in that other great conflict of the twentieth century. However, over a hundred years after the events described in this book, it is still possible to find small parts of the L33 in museums and collections, including a section of the framework on permanent display in the parish church of Little Wigborough, barely 500 metres from where the mighty airship fell to earth in the early hours of 24th September 1916.

Count von Zeppelin's first airship, the LZ-1, 128 metres in length, equivalent to the wingspan of two jumbo jets, first took to the skies over Lake Constance on 2 July 1900. From the lessons gained from this first prototype, the Zeppelin Company would progressively develop their airship capabilities so that 130 rigid airships would be constructed over the next forty years. The wealth of experience gained in the construction and operation of rigid airships by the Zeppelin Company resulted in Germany being the only nation with the capability to employ large rigid airships. In the years prior to the outbreak of the First World War, Zeppelin airships carried over 35,000 fee-paying passengers in flights covering 170,000 miles without any serious accidents, which was a remarkable achievement given that the technology involved was still in its infancy. Compared to the aeroplane, a journey by airship appeared to be a much safer form of travel. Given the airship's capabilities, it was little wonder that first, the German army and then the German navy showed considerable interest in developing the airship as a weapon of war. The military's reasoning was that the airships' very long endurance and lift-carrying capabilities, compared to the primitive aeroplanes of the day, could give them a reconnaissance and aerial bombardment capability superior to that possessed by potential adversaries, most notably France, Great Britain and Russia.

The Zeppelin Company was not the sole manufacturer of rigid airships employed by the German military during the First World War, although. However, during the conflict, the press and the British public would refer to all enemy airships as "Zeppelins." The Schutte-Lanz company built plywood rather than aluminium alloy framed airships. They were used in small numbers by both the army and the navy, with only 2% of bombing raids over Britain being made by airships of this type.

At the commencement of the First World War, the German navy possessed just one operational Zeppelin, the L3 (L1 and L2, the first two Navy Zeppelins having been lost in accidents), although more would soon follow off the production line. The primary role of the Zeppelin during the early months of the conflict was reconnaissance in support of the High Seas Fleet. As the Imperial German Navy had a significant numerical inferiority to the British Grand Fleet, it was hoped that intelligence gained by the scouting Zeppelins would give advanced warning of the Royal Navy's intentions and hence a tactical advantage in any ensuing conflict between the fleets.

The campaign of aerial bombardment of Britain began on 19 January 1915, having been approved by the Kaiser two weeks earlier. The first targets attacked were Great Yarmouth, Sheringham and King's Lynn, by the Zeppelins L3 and L4 (although their intended target had been the river Humber). Over the next three years, bombing campaigns would be launched primarily against Britain but also on Paris and other cities. Initially, the bombing was limited to military targets on the Kaiser's orders. Official British estimates list 498 civilians and 58 soldiers killed by air attacks in Britain between 1915 and 1918. 1,913 injuries are recorded. The Imperial Navy's Airships dropped 360,000 kg of bombs, the majority on the British Isles. 307,315 kg were directed at enemy vessels, ports, and towns; 58,000 kg were dropped over Italy, the Baltic, and the Mediterranean. German army airships carried 160,000 kg of bombs to their designated targets: 44,000 kg hit Belgium and France, 36,000 kg to England, and 80,000 kg to Russia and South-Eastern Europe.

Ultimately, the strategic bombing campaign of Britain by airships was a costly failure both economically and militarily. Given their immense size and relatively low speeds, they could, without undue difficulty, be kept illuminated by searchlights, creating a large target for anti-aircraft guns and attacking fighter aircraft. The highly inflammable hydrogen gas, from which they gained their buoyancy, also made them increasingly vulnerable, especially once the British developed explosive machine gun ammunition. The weather, too, played its part. In even a fairly gentle breeze, it was a highly labour labour-intensive and often hazardous exercise to manoeuvre a Zeppelin in and out of its protective shed, and many a mission was curtailed when stronger than forecast winds were encountered on the way to the target. Throughout the war, on average, on one day, five naval airships were unable to undertake patrols over the North Sea due to adverse weather. As Britain's air defences became more formidable, the Zeppelins were forced to higher altitudes to decrease their vulnerability, which made target identification and bombing accuracy more difficult, complex and inevitably less effective. Of the 84 German airships that took part in raids over Britain during World War 1, 30 were either shot down or destroyed in accidents.

Part one of this short book tells the story of one particular airship, the L33, from its construction at Friedrichshafen on the shores of Lake Constance to its fiery demise on the fateful night of September 23rd/24th, 1916.

Part two is a brief history of the subsequent Zeppelin bombing campaign during the remainder of the war.

Part 1

Chapter 1

The L33 was the fourth of the L30 series of Zeppelins, known to the allies as Super-Zeppelins. The L30 series was considered technically the most successful of all the Zeppelins built during WW1. In fact, such was the regard in which they were held that rigid airships built post-war by both Britain and the United States were virtually copies of the L30 class or its derivatives.

Zeppelin 'R' Type

Zeppelins in this class: L30, L31, L32, L33, L34, L35, L36, L37, L38, L39, L40, L41, L45, L47, L50

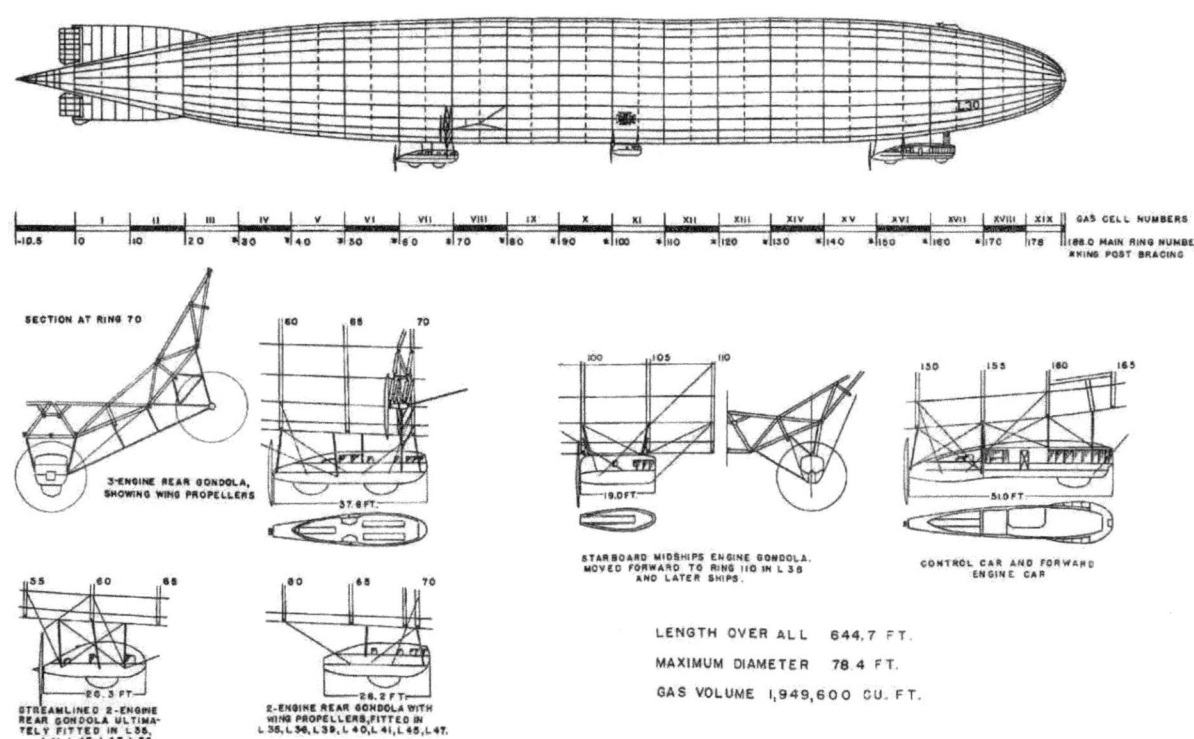

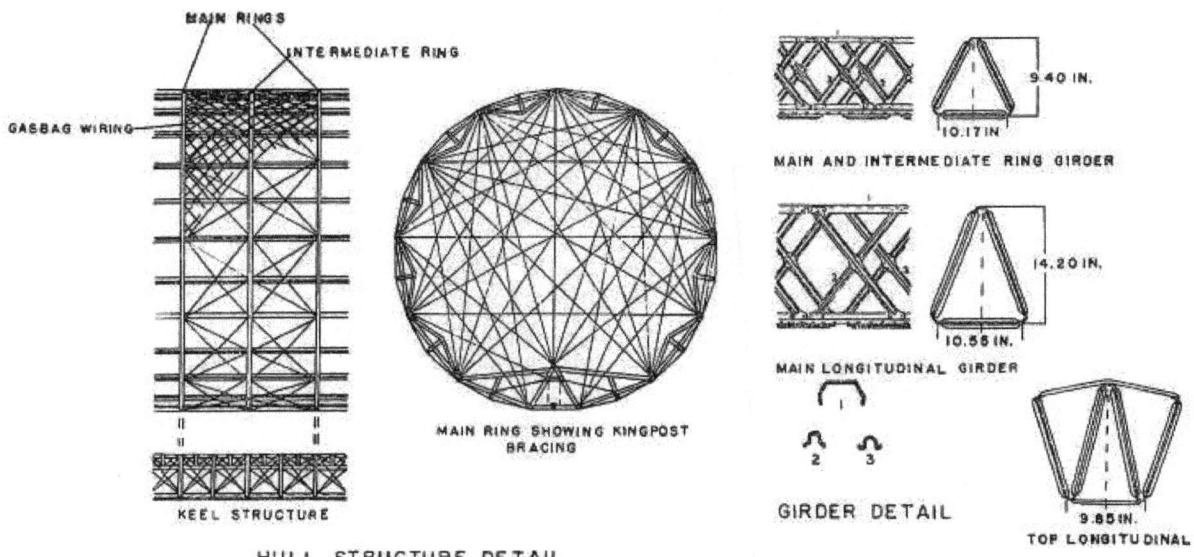

HULL STRUCTURE DETAIL

The L30 class was the first airship to boast a volume exceeding six million cubic feet (57000 cubic metres). With a length of 198 metres and a maximum diameter of 23.9 metres, the airships could reach a speed of 28.7 metres/second (64.2 miles per hour), powered by six 240 horsepower six-cylinder petrol-driven engines. The weight of the airship was over 31 metric tonnes, but once the 19 gas cells were filled with buoyant hydrogen, the airship was able to climb, under favourable conditions, to an altitude of 3,900 metres (12,800 feet). Even at that altitude, the airship, when viewed from the ground, would be an impressive sight, with its apparent length being approximately six times greater than the width of a full moon as seen from ground level. Offensively, the airship could carry almost 5 tons of bombs, and to provide protection from attack by aircraft, the airship carried machine guns located atop the forward hull, at the tail and in the gondolas below the hull.

The L33 was built in Factory Shed 1 at the Zeppelin works at Friedrichshafen, on the shores of Lake Constance on Germany's southern border, and completed on 30th August 1916. The building process began with constructing the circular transverse frames, which were then suspended 10 metres apart from the factory roof, while 13 longitudinal girders were added to provide the basic framework. A further 12 intermediate girders gave additional support to the structure and also helped to support the fabric covering which enveloped the whole airship. Within this tubular structure were inserted numerous steel bracing wires which contributed to the airship's strength and rigidity. The metal used throughout the structure was aluminium-based alloy duralumin, developed in Germany in 1908. It possessed a strength between two and a half and five times greater than pure aluminium of the same weight. To make the 19 gas cells, it has been estimated, required the intestines of 250,000 cows. The outer membranes of the intestines were soaked in a dilute solution of potassium hydroxide, washed, stretched, beaten flat and treated chemically to prevent putrefaction. Layers of the material were then glued together and then fashioned into a strong and flexible material which, most importantly, could safely contain the inflammable hydrogen gas that provided the airship with its buoyancy. This material, known as gold beater's skin, had long been used in the process of making gold leaf and had been found by experiment since the early days of ballooning in the late 18th century to be one of the very few materials that could hold hydrogen gas without serious leakage. To construct the gas cells, the gold beater's skin was attached by gluing to an inner layer of single-ply cotton fabric to provide strength. Despite this composite material being the best means of containing hydrogen then available, the continual slow loss of the gas by diffusion was a constant problem that airship commanders faced. Tests carried out by British technicians on samples from L33's gas cells recorded that the loss of hydrogen through the goldbeater skin amounted to about 1.3 litres per square metre per 24 hours. Such was the demand by the airship industry for gold beater's skin during the First World War, that the German government implemented restrictions on the production of bratwurst and other types of sausage.

To the underside of the framework were attached the control and engine gondolas which housed the six engines that powered the airship. Even given the war footing of the German economy, the speed at which the L33 was constructed was impressive. The design of the L30 series was begun in April 1915, and only six months later, on 30th August 1916, L33 was able to successfully complete her maiden flight. The Zeppelin airship programme was a significant cost to the German military expenditure. L33's price was 2.8 million Deutschmark, equivalent to about 10 million pounds in today's money.

For her maiden flight at Friedrichshafen, L33 was commanded by Baumeister Lau of the Zeppelin Company and was operated by a civilian crew. The trial flight was observed from the ground by reporters from the local press, together with naval ratings who were presumably eager to watch the brand-new airship put through her paces. After the flight, the airship's small, coracle-like lifeboat was tested by the future crew, who possibly harboured doubts as to whether such a small vessel could protect them should the airship have to ditch in a stormy sea.

L33 was commissioned on 2 September 1916, when her new captain, Kapitänleutnant der Reserve Aloys Böcker. Böcker, 37, was a career naval officer, having joined the Imperial German Navy in 1896. He was an experienced airship commander who had captained Zeppelins L5 and L14 and was a veteran of over a dozen raids. Much was expected from the new L30 series of Zeppelins, being able to fly both faster and higher and carry a larger bomb load than the airships that had preceded them. The Chief of the German Naval Airship Division, Fregattenkapitan Peter Strasser, was optimistic that these new additions to the fleet would play a significant role in the ultimate defeat of Britain. On the same day as L33 completed her maiden flight, Strasser wrote to Reinhard Scheer, commander in chief of the German High Seas Fleet:

"The performance of the big airships has reinforced my conviction that England can be overcome by means of airships, in as much as the country will be deprived of the means of existence though increasingly extensive destruction of cities, factory complexes, dockyards, harbour works with war and merchant ships lying therein, railroads, etc."

Up to the autumn of 1916 Zeppelins and the wooden constructed Schutt-Lanz airships had been able to roam with relative impunity through the night skies over Britain. Anti-aircraft fire often could not reach the airship's altitude and generally lacked accuracy. The other means of defence, fighter aircraft, struggled to climb to the required height, by which time the airship, with a similar speed to the attacking fighter, would be well out of range. Furthermore, it was found that despite the combustibility of hydrogen, the airships proved frustratingly difficult to fatally damage by machine gun fire. Even the incendiary ammunition of the time, despite repeatedly penetrating the airships' gas cells, failed to cause the hydrogen to ignite. Due to the combined effects of the British blackout, primitive navigation and unpredictable weather, the results of the bombing were limited. Bombs were scattered far and wide throughout the British countryside, and casualties had been comparatively light.

By the autumn of 1916, Germany's war machine was coming under increasing pressure. In May, the High Seas Fleet had inflicted heavy losses on the Royal Navy at the Battle of Jutland but had failed to loosen the stranglehold of the Royal Navy's blockade of shipping reaching German ports. On land, the offensive at Verdun designed to destroy the French army through a war of attrition had long since stalled, and the German army was struggling to contain the combined British and French offensive which ground inexorably forward on the Somme. On the eastern front, Germany's ally, the Austro-Hungarians, needed increasing assistance as their forces crumbled under the weight of Russia's Brusilov offensive. To further add to Germany's problems, Romania, on whom Germany had depended for oil as well as some food imports, had on August 14 entered the war on the side of the Allies.

In order to break this stalemate and provide an impetus to Germany's pursuit of victory, the Imperial Naval Airship Division would be required to inflict damaging blows on the British capital. Throughout the autumn months of 1916, against increasingly effective British defences and steadily worsening weather, the commander of the Naval Airship Division, Peter Strasser, ordered his airships to attack London. To bolster his forces, Strasser requested from Scheer an additional four airships (plus crews), increasing the number available to 22. In his letter to Scheer, Strasser wrote:

"I am well aware of the generally prevailing personnel problems, but I believe that the personnel must be made available, if necessary through reduction in other areas since the airships offer a certain means of victoriously ending the war".

Whether Strasser's optimism was shared by his commander is open to question, as on the margin of this, Scheer wrote, 'We will have to wait and see.' Yet despite possible misgivings, Scheer gave Strasser his full support.

The new aerial offensive on Britain began in earnest during the first week of August, around the time of the new moon. The effectiveness of these raids was, however, from a German perspective disappointing. At the mercy of the weather and with rudimentary navigation, airships scattered their bombs over an area ranging from Berwick to Dover, at a cost to the enemy of just over £1000 worth of damage. With low clouds and morning mists obscuring the ground, most bombs fell harmlessly in open countryside, to such an extent that the British authorities began to question whether there was a concerted plan to diminish Britain's harvest through deliberate bombing with incendiaries.

Much greater success was, however, achieved by Zeppelin L24 on the night of 8-9 August 1916 when Hull was attacked. The raid killed 10 civilians and caused over £13000 worth of damage.

Coinciding with the period of the next new moon, thirteen airships attacked southern England on the night of Wednesday-Thursday 23-24 August. Strasser himself was aboard the L32, the recently commissioned sister ship to the L33. Forewarned of the impending raid through intercepted wireless traffic, the Royal Navy put to sea the Harwich-based cruisers HMS Canterbury, Carysfort and Conquest, together with a number of destroyers hoping to engage the airships in daylight. As the line of warships sailed eastwards, a number of the airships were spotted, and at least six of them reported being attacked by naval gunfire. L13 was struck by a shell but no fire resulted, and the airship-made it safely back to her base, helped by a strong tailwind. This strong south-westerly to north-westerly wind severely slowed the progress of the remaining airships to such an extent that the English coast could not be reached before the moon rose at 2 am. Consequently, five of the airships turned back. Struggling against the headwind and heavily weighed down by rain, both L23 and L21, together with the wooden-built SL9, all sustained damage on landing, putting them out of service for some days.

Greater success, though, was achieved by Kapitänleutnant Heinrich Mathy and Oberleutnant Werner Peterson, commanding L31 and L32, respectively. They managed to avoid the Royal Navy's surface ships and the worst of the headwind by following a southerly course towards Aachen before turning westward via Brussels towards the Channel. Over Belgium, Mathy chose to fly at a lower altitude than Peterson, enabling his airship to remain hidden in the clouds from allied aeroplanes. Peterson, flying above the cloud, met stronger headwinds, slowing his progress to such an extent that he did not reach the English coast near Folkestone until around 2 a.m., too late to bomb London. Peterson, therefore, emptied his bomb load over various vessels lying off Dover. Most of the bombs fell harmlessly. With his bomb load gone, Peterson turned for home, avoiding the anti-aircraft fire from guns both onshore and at sea. He was briefly pursued by an aircraft from Dover, which managed to fire a drum load of machine gun ammunition towards the airship from below, seemingly to no ill effect. Uncertain of his position on the journey home, Peterson inadvertently steered his ship above or close to Dutch territorial waters and was heavily fired on by Dutch guns. Despite these mishaps, Peterson was able to land L32 undamaged at Nordholz at 08.30 a.m. Having reached the English coast several hours before Peterson, Mathy followed the Thames all the way to London. Once over the capital, Mathy was able to exploit the cloud and mist to periodically hide from guns and searchlights whilst delivering his deadly bomb load. In addition to a hit on a power station in Deptford, many houses were struck, leading to nine fatalities and forty wounded. The total damage caused was estimated at £130,000.

On the night of Saturday-Sunday, 2-3 September, the twelve airships sent out by Strasser were joined by four army airships. For the only time in the war, the Navy and Army would be bombing the same target simultaneously. In terms of the number of airships involved, it was the greatest raid of the war. The raid, however, was doomed to failure and marked a turning point in the campaign to subdue Britain by aerial bombardment.

Battling against adverse winds and belts of rain, and increasing snow at higher altitudes, a number of the airships struggled to maintain height as they became encrusted with ice. As a consequence, two of the raiders, L17 and the Army airship LZ97, both turned for home before reaching the enemy coast. Due to the combination of challenging weather and increasingly effective home defences, only a small proportion of the combined 32-ton bomb load carried by the 16 airships fell on the intended target, London. Bombs were scattered widely over the Home Counties and East Anglia. A sight that may well have inhibited the airships' commanders from pressing home their attacks was the fiery destruction of the Army airship SL-11, the first enemy airship to be shot down on British soil. The destroyer of the SL-11 was the 21-year-old Lieutenant William Leefe Robinson, who, for his actions that night, was awarded the Victoria Cross. Leefe Robinson, flying a BE 2c converted night fighter, was one of six pilots who had taken off in order to intercept the raiding airships. With a top speed of just over 70 mph, the BE 2c would take over 45 minutes to reach the airship's altitude.

Leefe Robinson had taken off from Sutton's Farm airfield near Hornchurch in Essex, where his squadron, No 39 (Home Defence), was based. His eventual victim, the SL-11, had crossed the coast by the River Crouch and then passed by the east of London, sweeping around in a large arc in order to attack the capital from the north. Bombs were dropped liberally over a number of northern London suburbs. By the time SL-11 reached Tottenham, she had come under heavy fire from the anti-aircraft guns of north and central London; the gunners' task was greatly assisted by the probing searchlights based at Finsbury Park and Victoria Park. Undoubtedly, it was the combined effect of searchlight beams and exploding anti-aircraft shells that drew the attention of three of the Royal Flying Corps fighters piloted by Lieutenants Leefe Robinson, Mackay and Hunt. The trio gave chase, with Leefe Robinson, being closest, arriving first on the scene. Despite the danger presented by the anti-aircraft shells bursting around his aircraft, he pressed home his attack, as this extract from his combat report relates.

At 2.05 a.m., a Zeppelin was picked up by searchlights over north east London (as far as I could judge). Remembering my last failure, I sacrificed height (I was still at 12,900ft) for speed and made my nose down toward the Zeppelin. I saw shells bursting and night tracer shells flying around it. When I drew closer, I noticed that the anti-aircraft aim was too high or too low; also, a good many, some 800ft behind – a few tracers went right over. I could hear the bursts when about 3,000ft from the Zeppelin. I flew about 800ft below it from bow to stern and distributed one drum along it (alternate New Brock and Pomeroy). It seemed to have no effect; I therefore, moved to one side and gave it another drum distributed along its side – without apparent effect. I then got behind it (by this time, I was very close -500ft or less below) and concentrated on one part (underneath the rear). I was then at a height of 11,500ft when attacking the Zeppelin. I hardly finished the drum before I saw the part fired at glow. In seconds, the whole rear part was blazing. When the third drum was fired, there were no searchlights on the Zeppelin, and no antiaircraft was firing. I quickly got out of the way of the falling Zeppelin and, being very excited, fired off a few red Very's (sic) lights and dropped a parachute flare. Having very little oil and petrol left, I returned to Sutton's Farm, landing at 2.45 a.m.

The brightly blazing Sl-11 took almost two minutes to fall to earth, its fiery glow clearly visible to many of the other airships making their way toward London. It must have been a fearfully ominous sight to their crews. The flaming remains of the Schutte-Lanz-built airship landed at Cuffley, in Hertfordshire, where, having a framework of wood rather than an aluminium alloy as in the case of Zeppelins, it continued to burn for nearly two hours. Only once the fire had burnt out could the badly burnt bodies of Hauptmann Wilhelm Schramm and his 15 crew members be recovered. Initially buried with full military honours at Potters Bar, their remains were re-interred at the Cannock Chase German Military Cemetery in 1962. Having mostly expended their bomb load, the remaining 15 airships all made it safely back to Germany, the last to land being L21, having been in the air for over 26 hours. Even without the loss of SL-11, the raid overall was a failure. Casualties inflicted were 4 killed and 12 injured, none of which were in the intended target of London, and monetary damage was estimated at £21,072. From the German perspective, though, the raid, at least from their public pronouncements, was regarded as a success. In a press release from Berlin, which was published in a number of European newspapers, it was stated that:

In addition to successfully targeting London, other Zeppelins attacked factories and fortifications at Norwich, where strong explosions and fires were caused. Searchlight batteries and industrial works in Oxford, Harwich, Boston and on the Humber were bombed, and numerous fires caused there. In Yarmouth the gas works and aerodromes were attacked and a battery silenced.

The loss of the SL-11 was not mentioned. Despite the optimistic tone of the press release, the German Army airship service never again attempted to raid England, and the service was disbanded within a year. Despite the withdrawal of the German Army airships from the fray, the German Navy airship service under the leadership of Strasser still exuded confidence. They would, however, have to wait until the following new moon period for the next opportunity to attack England. The forthcoming raid would mark the combat debut of the brand-new L33.

Chapter 2

Throughout the early afternoon of Saturday, 23rd September 1916, a total of eleven Zeppelins took off from their bases in Northwest Germany, with L33 being released from her mooring ropes at Nordholz at 1.24 p.m. Launching a Zeppelin was a painstaking process requiring considerable manpower. Nearly 700 ground troops were based at Nordholz, one of whose many tasks was to ease the giant airships from their sheds. In 1916, Nordholz was the largest German airship base, with three fixed sheds, each constructed on an approximately South-West/North-East orientation. In addition, Nordholz possessed a double shed, which, despite weighing 4,000 tonnes, was able to rotate. This was built so that the shed could be aligned with the wind prior to the Zeppelin being walked out. With a fixed shed, even a gentle cross wind could result in catastrophic damage during the delicate process of extracting the airship from its shed. Before launch, the Zeppelin would be fully laden, and the gas cells filled with hydrogen whilst still inside the shed but prevented from rising by the weight of numerous sandbags distributed evenly around the gondolas' guard rails. On the word of command these sandbags would be released simultaneously, whereupon the airship would become buoyant. If not, ballast would be slowly released until buoyancy was achieved. Böcker's executive officer, Leutnant Schirilitz, would then jump out, being simultaneously replaced by a similar-sized member of the ground crew, to prevent the airship from rising. Under orders from Schirilitz, the ground crew would secure the Zeppelin both fore and aft to rail-mounted trolleys and then a team of several hundred handlers would slowly walk out of the airship until she was well clear of the shed. To launch the Zeppelin, water ballast would be released, allowing her to rise. As altitude was gained, atmospheric pressure would fall, causing the gas cells to expand until automatic valves in the cells opened to allow some of the hydrogen to escape. Maintaining or changing altitude and keeping the airship trimmed required a balance of releasing ballast or manually venting off hydrogen, a task made more challenging should the airship become heavier due to rain or an accumulation of ice.

Mindful of the more effective anti-Zeppelin measures being afforded to London and the loss of SL-11 earlier in September, Strasser's plan for this latest raid was for the most advanced Zeppelins, L33, together with her sister ships L30, L31 and L32, to attack London, whereas the eight older airships would attack the less well defended Midlands. Of those eleven Zeppelins launched with such high expectations that afternoon, only nine would return.

As with previous Zeppelin raids on Britain the departure of the airships had not gone unnoticed. Radio call signs had been picked up by monitoring stations, and the signals were transcribed by the code breakers of room 40 of the Admiralty in Whitehall. In the space of a few hours, GHQ Home Forces had alerted the gun batteries, searchlight crews and home defence airfields to ensure they were at a state of readiness for the attack that was likely to follow.

Flying at an average speed of approximately 50 mph and maintaining an altitude of about 5,000ft, the Zeppelins took over nine hours to reach the English coast. After leaving Nordholz, Captain Aloys Böcker had taken L33 on a course following the German coast until east of Borkum before turning west to cross the North Sea towards England. On reaching the Thames estuary, she passed just to the North of the Black Deep light ship at around 22.00, when she was fired on by a destroyer in the Edinburgh Deep. The ship's crew had initially been alerted to her presence by the distinctive reverberating roar produced by the L33's six Maybach engines with their giant 17-foot diameter propellers. The naval gunners' fire was soon supported by land-based guns, although there is no evidence that any of the projectiles launched skywards left any mark on the airship. Successfully avoiding damage, the L33 flew over Foulness Point, the northernmost tip of Foulness Island, and after crossing the River Crouch, Böcker set a course of 265 degrees, directly towards London. At approximately 23.00, Böcker released the first of the sixty or so bombs carried in four bomb compartments on the underside of the airship, either side of the rear engine power cars. What Böcker was targeting remains unclear, as the bomb exploded harmlessly into fields just to the east of the village of Hockley. Pressing on towards the intended target of London at a speed of around 50 mph, the deep drone of the L33's six engines would have been clearly audible as she steadily made her way over the towns and villages of South Essex. Continuing on her course, taking her South of Battlesbridge and Wickford and then over Billericay, Böcker and his 21 crew members would have been at their stations in readiness for the hostile reception they would receive from the gun crews and fighter pilots that defended the capital, now buoyed by the spectacular destruction of the SL-11 barely three weeks previously. Against the barrage thrown up by the quick firing 3 inch anti-aircraft guns, which could fire up to 25 rounds per minute to an effective altitude of 25,000 ft, well beyond the altitude that the L33 could achieve, there was no defence, especially on such a clear starry night. To counter the threat posed by fighter aircraft, however, the L33 was defended by seven 7.92mm calibre Maxim Nordenfelt machine guns. Two of these were located in the forward control gondola, one in each of the two wing power cars, two in the gun platform positioned on the upper surface of the Zeppelin, above the nose, plus a single machine gun on a platform at the tail.

Eager to catch the defenders unawares, Böcker approached the metropolis at speed and, at about 23.30, shortly after passing over Billericay, he released a flare in an attempt to ascertain the airship's position but also to dazzle the gun batteries and searchlight crews. As the flare slowly descended on its parachute, taking about five minutes to fall to earth, the intense white light produced by the burning magnesium had the desired effect. The defenders could clearly hear that now familiar sound of the Zeppelin's engines, but while the flares burnt, their loss of night vision severely inhibited their ability to spot the airship against the starry background.

Aided by the light of the flare, Böcker released in quick succession four incendiary bombs, two of which fell on Argent Farm on Upminster Common, followed about ten minutes later by six high explosive bombs, four falling in the vicinity of Sutton's Farm aerodrome at Hornchurch, the same airfield from which Lt Leefe Robinson had taken off from the night he shot down the SL-11. Other than forming craters on the airfield, the bombs caused no damage. One of the bombs narrowly missed the farmhouse, and another fell close to a hanger. As aircraft were operating from the field in response to the Zeppelin threat, the runway's flares had been lit. They were rapidly extinguished as soon as the Zeppelin was spotted overhead.

Shortly before midnight, over Chadwell Heath, Böcker released a second flare, which again seriously inconvenienced the local searchlight crew. However, as the magnesium flare burned out, the airship became more visible and began to be picked up by searchlight crews probing the sky for the source of the menacing drone. Over Wanstead, Böcker then turned in a southerly direction, taking the L33 over the packed terrace houses of East Ham (see maps page 67-70). Five minutes later, as she approached the Royal Albert Dock, Böcker veered West again, passing between the now active guns at Beckton and North Woolwich. With the target approaching, Böcker gave the order for much of the remaining water ballast to be released in order to gain as much altitude as possible. Thus lightened, the L33 slowly climbed to 13,000 ft, although she remained well within the range of the guns below. As the L33 moved ever closer to the city, she was met by a barrage of fire from the West Ham gun, which opened up at 0010, whereupon Böcker, under the impression that he was in the vicinity of Tower Bridge (although he was actually about four miles to the North East) gave the order to begin releasing the L33's bomb load.

According to Böcker's report:

"Between 12.00 and 12.40, starting at Tower Bridge, two bombs of 300Kg, eight of 100kg, thirty-two of 50Kg and twenty incendiaries were dropped over the big warehouses along the Thames and over the City. Several enormous fires and the collapse of whole groups of houses were observed."

Where the bombs and incendiaries actually fell was among the tightly packed houses and businesses of Bromley-by- Bow and Stratford. One of the first bombs to be released fell close to the junction of Empson Street and St Leonard Street, with fatal consequences for six residents when a 100kg high explosive bomb detonated on impact, severely damaging four houses and shattering windows in many others. Eleven other residents were also injured. Just South of Empson Street lay the 17-acre site of Russia Wharf on the north bank of the Limehouse Cut. Among the incendiaries that fell here, it is thought that just three were responsible for setting fire to the timber store at the timber yard and sawmill of furniture makers W Lusty and Sons. Despite the heroic efforts of the Metropolitan Fire Brigade, it was estimated that 43,000 cubic feet of timber was incinerated. Almost simultaneously, a quarter of a mile to the south west, just to the North of the Limehouse Cut waterway, four high explosive bombs, one 300 Kg, one 100 Kg and two 50 Kg, struck the North London Railway Depot wrecking carriages and buildings, including a boiler house, as well as damaging the track. Fortunately, no one was killed or injured. Just to the South of the Limehouse Cut, the sprawling Spratt's factory complex on Morris Street had a fortunate escape when a 50 kg bomb exploded, forming a crater that exposed the foundations but otherwise did no damage. Just a minute or two later, and about a mile further north, another 50 kg bomb extensively damaged the Baptist Chapel that stood on the corner of Devons Road and Botolph Road. Although no injuries were inflicted here, just two streets away, barely a hundred or so yards to the north, fatalities did result from the 100 Kg bomb that struck the Black Swan public house on the corner of Bow Road and Bromley High Street. The blast from the explosion ripped through the building taking out all floors right through to the cellar. The landlord, George Reynolds' two daughters, Cissie Reynolds and Sylvia Adams, aged 20 and 21, respectively, were killed together with Sylvia's thirteen month-old daughter and their grandmother Mrs Potter. Eight-year-old George Reynolds and his nine -year-old brother Sydney, along with Sylvia's husband, Henry Adams, were injured. Such was the ferocity of the blast that the neighbouring premises were also seriously damaged, and the nearby County Council School on the corner of Bromley High Street and Devons Road had its windows blown out. In addition to the casualties at the Black Swan, four men, two women and a child living in the vicinity also sustained injuries. Moving north and crossing over Bow Road, the L33's next 100 kg bomb exploded close to the junction of Old Ford Road and Wrexham Road. Other than some blown-out windows, little damage to property was inflicted, although three women sustained injuries. Turning to the north-east and passing over Bow Creek towards Stratford, the Zeppelin dropped a 100 Kg bomb on Edward Cook and Company's soap works but only minor damage resulted as the bomb failed to explode. Continuing in a north-easterly direction, two further high-explosive bombs caused severe damage to the British Petroleum depot (formerly the Homelight Oil Company depot prior to 1912) at the end of Marshgate Lane. A concrete wall was demolished, underground oil pipes and an 18-inch water pipe were ruptured, and part of a sewer bank washed away. The blast from the explosions blew out numerous windows in the surrounding industrial buildings. Despite the extensive damage, there were no casualties, although the fires from burning oil drums took the hard-pressed Metropolitan Fire Brigade several hours to extinguish. The Zeppelin's final bombs to fall on London were seven 50 Kg bombs and some incendiaries, which fell around a third of a mile further to the north east in the vicinity of G M Judd and Brothers' match factory on Carpenters Road. The resulting fires consumed much of the building and most of the stock.

The effect of a 50kg high explosive bomb on the Baptist chapel in Botolph Road, Bow.

The explosion damaged, to varying degrees, twenty-three shops and houses on Botolph Road. There was further damage in Devons Road. Two children, Symon Goldman and Ely Goldman, aged 13 and 11, were both injured by shock.

Whilst Böcker was unleashing his cargo of destruction, the L33 was clearly illuminated by a number of searchlight beams, to the considerable benefit of the gunners below. As she made her journey northwards, the West Ham gun was joined by guns at Beckton, Victoria Park and Wansted. The West Ham crew, with their Vickers 3-pounder quick-firing gun, were able to fire eighteen rounds in two minutes, beating the Wansted crew, who managed eleven rounds in three minutes. The Victoria Park crew managed to fire seven rounds in a minute before their guns jammed. The ferocity of the gunfire was greater than either Böcker or his crew had ever experienced. A veteran of eight previous raids over England, Böcker later wrote:

"The gunfire from all sides was extraordinarily heavy, more so than I had ever experienced."

Chief Machinist's mate Adolf Schultz, looking out through a ventilation hatch from a position amidships whilst crouching on the narrow catwalk that ran the length of the Zeppelin, counted thirty searchlights, many of which now held the airship in their dazzling white beams, from which there was seemingly no escape.

The crew of the L33 were increasingly desperate to unload their bombs and to escape from the probing searchlights and increasingly accurate gunfire. The forty or so minutes spent releasing their bomb load on the streets and terrace houses of Bow and Bromley, as shells burst all around them, must have seemed much longer. Given the intensity of the anti-aircraft fire, the amount of time that the Zeppelin was within range and the sheer size of the target it presented meant that the chance of the L33 escaping unscathed was very slim. Over Bromley, an artillery shell, thought to be either from the guns at Beckton or Wansted, entered through the underside of the L33, about 20 metres or so to the rear of the control car. It either exploded inside the airship or possibly traversed through it and exited through the upper surface. Either way, the damage caused was catastrophic and dealt a fatal blow to the Zeppelin's chances of ever returning home. The shell destroyed gas cell 14, fractured main ring 120 and severed the ship's axial cable, weakening the structure. Another near miss also certainly damaged at least one of the Zeppelin's six giant propellers, causing a change to the distinctive pulsating engine noise, widely reported by witnesses below. As well as the rapid loss of hydrogen from cell 14, gas also vented into the atmosphere from the numerous rents and tears in adjacent cells, caused by shrapnel and shredded aluminium girders. Exposed to a hail of shrapnel from other near misses, many of the Zeppelin's 19 gas cells were punctured, adding to the loss of hydrogen, without which the airship was doomed.

Paintings by Felix Schwormstadt give an impression of life aboard a Zeppelin on operations.

Miraculously, the highly inflammable hydrogen did not catch fire, but rapidly losing buoyancy, the airship began to descend at an uncontrolled rate, falling over 3,000 feet in four minutes. In a desperate effort to maintain altitude, the last of the water ballast was released, which, when illuminated by the Kelvedon Hatch searchlight, was interpreted as a 'smoke screen' by the searchlight crew below. As the helmsmen steered the mortally wounded Zeppelin away from the searchlights and guns towards the Essex coast, members of the crew climbed throughout the cavernous structure in a desperate effort to stem the flow of leaking hydrogen. Working in darkness with only a few torches to guide them, they frantically sealed up what punctures they could find using patches held on with cellulose dope, hastily applied using brushes. It was a most hazardous task. Clambering through the maze of girders and bracing wire, many hands suffered cuts from the jagged edges of the duralumin latticework, and at least one crew member was nearly overcome by the fumes of the toxic dope.

As the crew of the L33 fought desperately to save their airship, they were unaware that another threat to their chances of survival was approaching in the form of a BE2c fighter aircraft, number 4544 of Number 39 Home Defence Squadron, piloted by New Zealander Second Lieutenant Alfred de Bathe Brandon. Brandon, a lawyer in peace time, qualified as a pilot at his own expense in October 1915 at Hall Flying School Hendon before joining The Royal Flying Corps in December of the same year. Brandon had gained considerable experience in the hazardous pursuit of night flying, having previously attacked Zeppelin L15 in March. On this night, Brandon took off from Hainault Farm airfield at 23.30, at about the same time the L33 was releasing incendiary bombs over Upminster, some eight miles to the south-east. His orders were to patrol between Hainault and Sutton Farm airfield, Hornchurch. Brandon had been on patrol for about 40 minutes when he spotted the L33, illuminated by the searchlights, as Böcker was beginning to drop the first of the bombs on Bromley-by-Bow. Immediately, he steered towards his quarry, but with a top speed of 70 mph, giving a likely closing speed of around 20 mph, it was not until the L33 was well clear of London, over Kelvedon Hatch, that Brandon was able to open fire. His report describes the attack:

At 12.12, I saw a Zeppelin in the searchlight some distance away and made for it. Very shortly after this, it escaped from the searchlights, and I lost it, but I continued on and picked it up again. I went on climbing and managed with some difficulty to keep it in view, as there were no searchlights on it, and my automatic pump had failed and I had to work the cockpit handle of the Lewis gun. After putting on a drum of ammunition, I came up behind the Zeppelin and, on raising the gun, jerked it out of the mounting, the gun and yoke falling across the nacelle. I managed to replace the gun but, in the meantime had passed under and past the Zepp. I turned and passed along it again, but from the bow, we passed each other too quickly for me to aim. On turning, I came up from behind the Zepp and fixed a drum of ammunition. The Brock seemed to be bursting all along it but the Zepp did not catch fire. I was using Brock, Pomeroy and Sparklet. I turned again and put on a fresh drum and came up behind and fired again. The gun jammed after about nine rounds. I now decided to get above the Zepp and went on climbing, but there was a large bank of clouds all around the horizon, and it was impossible to see the Zepp against it after I got level with Zepp. I first saw the Zepp at 12.13 and lost it at 12.33. I continued to patrol in various directions, having lost my bearings. I was about 10,200 feet when attacking the Zepp, and I should say the Zepp was about 1,000 to 1,200 feet higher.

As cloud and darkness swallowed the wounded airship and with his fuel running low, Brandon's only option was to return to Hainault Farm. The failure to bring about the fiery destruction of the Zeppelin must have been particularly frustrating for Brandon. Just under six months earlier, he had attacked the L15 over Ingatestone with machine fire and explosive darts. Despite pressing home his attacks from close range whilst coming under machine gun fire from the crew manning the upper gun platform, the Zeppelin had refused to burn. As the L15 turned for the coast, Brandon lost contact, but already depleted of hydrogen from anti-aircraft damage; the airship never made it home. She came down in the sea off Margate. For his bravery in attacking the L15, Brandon was awarded the Military Cross. The Distinguished Service Order was his reward for his attempt to destroy the L33.

Brandon's shooting had been good. His rounds had penetrated the gas cells and a number had ruptured fuel tanks. The nitroglycerine-containing Pomeroy ammunition was designed to explode on striking the outer covering of a Zeppelin, which would then ignite the escaping hydrogen. If this did not immediately occur, then the explosive Brock round, containing potassium chlorate, should have the same effect. The Sparklet ammunition was a tracer round, enabling Brandon to visually follow his shooting onto the target. The Brock and Pomeroy ammunition had been developed explicitly for anti-Zeppelin purposes following numerous failed attempts by fighters to destroy airships in the air. Although the new ammunition proved more successful, as was shown by Leefe Robinson's downing of the SL-11, throughout the remainder of the war, Zeppelins continued to prove frustratingly challenging to ignite, despite being filled with highly inflammable, and when mixed with air, highly explosive hydrogen. The explanation was that the airship's hydrogen gas cells were at a pressure only slightly higher than the surrounding air so that when the gas cell was punctured by a round, the gas only escaped gradually. This meant that the proportion of hydrogen in the air when the explosive round detonated was insufficient for combustion to occur.

2nd Lt Alfred de Bathe Brandon

L33's Commander Kapitanleutnant Alois Böcker

Fregettenkapitan Peter Strasser, Chief of the Naval Airship Service

Preoccupied with their frantic efforts to save their airship, the crew would, in many cases, have been unaware of Brandon's attacks. The gunners positioned in their lofty position on top of the hull saw the approaching fighter but, mindful of the hydrogen streaming from the ruptured gas cells, did not return fire for fear of the conflagration that might have followed.

Desperate to slow the rate of descent, Böcker employed the Zeppelin's massive elevators to raise the nose in order to generate some aerodynamic lift, but the effects were minimal. With the airship at this unnatural angle, the crew would have struggled to avoid sliding aft. With no more ballast on board and all bombs gone, there was only one remaining option if the airship was to remain buoyant, which was to throw out anything and everything that was not essential.

Chapter 3

As the L33 continued its slow descent across the Essex landscape below, the crew worked feverishly to lighten their craft. Over the following days, the L33's path became clearly apparent from the trail of jetsam strewn across the fields, stretching from just north of Chelmsford to Witham. Among the objects found over the following days, and then with a few exceptions dutifully handed into the authorities by their finders, were Maxim machine guns, together with cartridge boxes, revolvers, toolboxes and assorted tools and spare parts, as well as Bosch magnetos, parachute flares, an aluminium stool, torches, maps and even a four-gallon can of coffee. The first of the discarded machine guns was found at Boreham. Böcker also ordered surplus oil and petrol to be discarded, leaving just sufficient reserves, in the hope of making it across the North Sea. At half past midnight, radio operator Peter Morsdorf sent the L33's final, desperate radio message: 'Need help mouth of Thames, L33'. Very shortly afterwards, the Telefunken radio transmitter was broken up and thrown overboard. The fragments of the radio were swiftly followed by three more machine guns, one falling at Monkton's House at Wickham Bishops and two more on Gate House Farm Tiptree, one of which landed in a crop of lucerne and was only found four days later. The guns mounted on the upper gun platform were only kept on board due to the impossibility of throwing them over the side. Despite each gun weighing nearly 30 Kg, their loss did little to slow the Zeppelin's descent. By the time the L33 was passing over the Kelvedon to Tollesbury branch line, just South of Tolleshunt Major, its altitude was down to perhaps a few hundred feet. Despite the incessant pounding from the six Maybach engines with their giant whirling propellers, the crew's shouts and barked orders as they battled to keep their craft airborne could be clearly heard from the ground below. With the airship's bow pointing ever upwards in a vain effort to gain some aerodynamic lift, the Zeppelin now barely responded to the helmsmen's controls as they battled to contend with the South Easterly wind on her beam. On reaching the coast at the mouth of the River Blackwater Estuary, Böcker was faced with a terrible dilemma; whether to proceed out to sea and almost certainly drown, along with his crew, or to turn inland and face captivity. Possibly following consultation with his fellow officers, Böcker chose the latter. Barely under control and driven by the wind, the dying airship passed over Mersea Island, crossed the Strood Channel and then at approximately 01.20 hours, still in an exaggerated tail-down orientation, she stalled, and her tail struck the ground. Then, a gust of wind dragged the Zeppelin another hundred or so yards until she finally came to rest in fields of stubble in the village of Little Wigborough, by pure chance narrowly missing New Hall Cottages. The airship lay across the hawthorn hedges that bordered Copt Hall Lane, its front third lying in Glebe Field with the remainder in the Napp Field. The weatherboarded New Hall Cottages barely lay 25 yards from the airship's starboard beam.

The heavy landing broke the airship's back, the braced aluminium framework giving way in several places. There was a small explosion, possibly in one of the gas cells, which did no damage other than burn off some of the Zeppelin's outer covering. The 30-ton structure, now virtually lacking in any buoyancy, crushed downwards on the gondolas beneath. Fearful of a fiery conflagration, the crew hastily made their escape, but despite the leaking petrol tanks and with hydrogen still seeping from torn gas cells, much to their huge relief, the ship still did not catch fire. Remarkably, other than a few cuts and bruises, no one was injured other than Maschinenmaat Arthur Franz Piepkorn, who fractured a rib as he fell heavily after jumping clear.

Gathering his crew together and establishing that everyone was accounted for, Böcker took stock of the situation. Mindful that his still largely intact airship would reveal to the British a treasure trove of technical details about the latest Zeppelin design, he decided that his only course of action was to destroy the L33 by fire and deny its secrets to the enemy. Böcker would have been aware that the British authorities, alerted by the very visible spectacle of the descending Zeppelin, might soon arrive to apprehend him and his crew, so it is to his credit that he sought to warn the occupants of the cottages before setting fire to the airship.

The New Hall Cottages were homes of farm labourers who worked at the nearby farm of the same name. In the left-hand cottage lived Thomas Lewis together with his wife and children. Their neighbours in the right-hand cottage were Frederick Choat and his family. Without a doubt, the families were in great trepidation, having witnessed the Zeppelin's crash landing and the crew gathering outside their homes. Böcker and his crew banged on doors and windows in an attempt to alert the families of the impending conflagration, but their pleas went unanswered. During the following days, Lewis gave interviews to a number of newspapers:

'It (referring to the explosion that occurred when the airship crash landed) didn't hurt any of us, but smashed the front windows of my house and those of my neighbours. I found afterwards that all the hair was singed off the back of my dog, which was in a kennel outside. Then, all that blessed crew came to my cottage and started knocking at the door. I never answered, and I heard

the commander cursing. He spoke English'. Asked if the German said *"Kamerad"* he replied. *'I don't know what else he said, but I put my wife and three children in the back room and made myself scarce too. The end of the airship dropped across the road which is by the cottage. I am glad I saw it and very glad too that I am alive now.'*

Having failed to persuade either the Choat or Lewis families to come out of their homes, Böcker ordered all of the L33's documents to be stashed in the wreckage of the control gondola prior to setting fire to the airship. As the crew moved clear Böcker fired a signal flare into the petrol-soaked walkway, igniting the fuel immediately. The flames spread rapidly, engulfing the entire airship within a matter of minutes. The intense heat ignited some machine gun ammunition and once the flames reached the gas cells, a series of three far greater explosions occurred from the traces of hydrogen, mixed with air, still remaining in the cells. The force of the blast was sufficient to knock over a number of the closer members of the crew and blow out several windows in the cottages. The cottages were also slightly shifted on their foundations and their paintwork scorched and blistered. Other than shock, no harm came to either the Choat or Lewis families other than the singed fur of the Lewis's white terrier.

Satisfied that there was nothing further that he or his crew could achieve by remaining, and with the crumpled and twisted framework still glowing, Böcker set off with his men along Copt Hall Lane, past New Hall Farm towards the main road. What their plans were remains a matter of conjecture to this day. Perhaps they were hoping to make their way to Mersea Island, steal a fishing boat and sail across the North Sea to Germany or occupied Belgium. However, the fact that the service pistols still in the crew members' possession were emptied and then discarded in the hedgerows, suggests they intended to give themselves up if apprehended, without resisting. Making their way along the lane, they passed through the darkened Grove Farm where their voices were heard by a 13 year old George Rout. Speaking many years later about the events he recalled:

'My mother kept saying, "the old Germans are coming up the road. I can hear them talking. Why don't you get yourself up, they'll burn the whole place down!" They passed our gate, all 21 of them, and was a big relief when they did get past.'

On reaching the main road, Böcker and his crew turned right in the direction of Peldon and Mersea Island beyond. It was a pitch black night, the waning moon not rising for another two hours. As the crew marched along the road, led by their captain, cycling towards them was Special Constable Edgar Nicholas, who, having been wakened by the explosions at about 01.20 had quickly arisen, dressed and then leaving his wife Flory and children behind, had ventured forth from his home in Peldon to investigate. As he pedalled towards Little Wigborough the flames from the burning Zeppelin glowed brightly ahead of him. At a left-hand bend in the road known as Kidhearts Corner, Special Constable Nicholas came face to face with Böcker and his crew. Dismounting his cycle and showing considerable calm and composure he shone his torch at the body of men before him and at Böcker in particular.

Special Constable Nicholas's account of what followed was given later that day to Captain M B D Ffinch, who reported his experience as follows:

I was in bed and heard an explosion about 1.20 a.m. this morning 24th September, 1916. I at once proceeded on my cycle towards Little Wigborough where I could see a fire. On arriving at Kidhearts Corner' Wigborough Road, Peldon, I met a company of men marching towards Peldon. I at once dismounted, addressing their leader asked, "Is it a Zeppelin down"? He said, "How many miles is it to Colchester"? I replied, "About 6". He replied, "Thank you". I at once recognised a foreign accent and from their clothing and conversation knew they were Germans. I received no answer to my questions. The men proceeded towards Peldon village, I followed walking with the rear men one of whom spoke broken English. I asked this man if he was hit with gun-fire. He answered, "Zeppelin explode. We crew prisoners of war". Later he remarked, "What people think of war". I replied, "I hardly know". He said, "Did I think (it was) nearly over". I replied, "It's over for you anyway". He answered, "Goot Goot", offering to shake my hand which I did. After this he gave me his lifesaving vest and a screw-hammer which he later informed me in good English was his revolver; with regard to the vest, he said, "Schwim Schwim", extending his arms in swimming fashion and added, "Souvenir. Commander speak English. I learn English at school".

When the party had reached Peldon Hall lower farm gate they were met by Special Constable Elijah Traylor, a bricklayer by trade, and by an off duty policeman Sergeant Ernest Edwards. Sergeant Edwards was from Hatfield Broad Oak, but was staying in a cottage just a few fields away from where the Zeppelin fell. He was familiar with Little Wigborough having married a girl from the village, Ida Ponder in the Village church, St Nicolas', five years previously. Sergeant Edwards took charge and led the group past Ransomes Farm and across Peldon Common to the Post Office where there was a telephone exchange, his intention being to contact the appropriate authorities, who would then relieve him of his prisoners. Given the lateness of the hour, he was perhaps surprised to find the exchange already manned by the village post mistress Mrs Fanny Smallwood together with the local police constable PC Charles Smith. Having seen the Zeppelin crash at a distance PC Smith had already alerted the authorities and was waiting for a return call, as he described in his report completed the following day:

"I beg to report about 1 a.m. on Sunday the 24th September 1916, a Zeppelin passed over Peldon flying very low in a South West course and appeared to be suffering with engine trouble. About 1.20.a.m. I last saw of her [sic] and almost immediately she burst into flames and there was a terrific explosion. I rang up Intelligence and informed them of the fact. While waiting to get on to Headquarters, Sergeant Edwards, who was on leave from Hatfield Broad Oak, came into the Post Office with the Commander of the Zeppelin".

Sergeant Edwards explained to the no doubt surprised P. C Smith that as well as the commander of the Zeppelin, the entire crew was outside, being guarded by Special constable Nicholas, who by now had been joined by Special Constables Percy Fairhead and Charles King. Edwards, who was strictly on leave, was perhaps eager to be relieved from any further responsibilities for the prisoners, so requested that Smith formally take charge of them, which he duly did. Sergeant Edwards then shortly afterwards returned to join his wife Ida, satisfied that he had done his duty, although much to his chagrin he was later officially rebuked by the Essex Chief Constable for having delegated responsibility for the prisoners to a more junior police officer.

Now clearly in charge, P. C Smith followed the instruction given in the official standing orders issued to the Police for situations such as this. He telephoned the nearest military unit, the Army post on Mersea Island, four miles away, to request an armed escort for the prisoners. After the call Böcker requested permission to use the telephone. This was flatly denied by Smith, who is reputed to have said "You certainly won't use this telephone". The policeman then ordered the Captain to wait outside with his men. Böcker's reason for wanting to use the phone was in all probability to formally surrender himself and crew to a senior military authority, rather than a local village policeman. However, the accounts of his request to telephone became somewhat embellished by journalists, the most widely reported fiction being that Böcker wished to contact his wife via a friend in London to inform her that he was safe. This version, which appeared in a number of contemporary accounts, and in some others since, was totally contradicted by Captain John Alfred Unett of the Essex County Constabulary. In his reply to the brigadier general of the Southern Army who had queried the accuracy of the PC Smith's reports, Captain Unett wrote:

There is no truth in the report that the captain of the German airship recently brought down at Little Wigborough asked to be allowed to telephone to a friend in London who would let his wife know he was safe. What appears to have happened is that captain asked the Constable if he might telephone but not saying where or to whom. I presume that the officer wanted to telephone to the military authorities.

On the assumption that the Army was on its way from West Mersea, but uncertain as to when they would arrive, PC Smith and the Special Constables, now seven in number, decided to escort their prisoners towards Mersea, with a view to handing over their charges on rendezvousing with the armed escort. With Smith leading the way and with the 'Specials', keeping a watchful eye over the Germans, the party set off, leaving behind the few onlookers who had by now gathered, staring in astonishment at the enemy who had appeared so unexpectedly in their midst. Edgar Nicholas was not part of the escort although his memorable night was far from over. He got back on his bicycle and pedalled his way over to the still smouldering skeleton of the L33 to keep watch until relieved.

About a mile before reaching the Strood, the road causeway that connects Mersea Island to the mainland, the group were met by an armed escort of four soldiers who had come from Mersea with orders to take charge of the prisoners. However, as there was no officer present, P C Smith refused to immediately surrender his captives. Eventually on reaching the Strood, they were met by Colonel Awell's 83rd Provisional Detachment, to whom Smith was satisfied to relinquish responsibility for the Captain and crew of L33. Finally relieved of their charges the policemen made their back to Peldon, their duty done. Later in his report Smith described the handover of prisoners:

There (at the Strood) I met Colonel Oevee and said to him, 'I have the crew of the wrecked Zeppelin here sir'. He said, 'How many have you?' I said, I don't know Sir, but with your permission I will count them.' Which I did and found there were 21 all told. I was assisted with [sic] Special Constables Fairhead, Clement Hyam, Charles King, Elijah Traylor, Joseph May, Horace Charles Meade, Harry Beard, and Edgar Nicholas. I have since made enquiries and find that the Zeppelin landed quite safe near New Hall cottages, Little Wigborough. It appears after the Zeppelin landed, the crew knocked at the doors of the cottages close by and they were heard to say. 'The wind lays right' and then they fired her.

In recognition of his actions that night PC Charles Smith was both promoted to Sergeant and awarded a coveted Merit Star that same day by Captain Unett, the Essex Chief Constable. Force orders of 24th September stated that:

'PC Smith is promoted Sergeant and awarded the Merit Badge for coolness and judgement, in handing over to the Military Authorities the Commander and crew of a Zeppelin....'

The service of the special constables that night and over the coming days was also recognised. Just over two months later, on Saturday 2nd December in a ceremony at Colchester Town Hall, Special Constables Edgar Nicholas, The Reverend E G Bowring, Joseph May, Charles King, Harry Beard, Elijah Traylor, Tom Wyncoll, Clement Hyam, Percy Fairhead, and Corporal J W Wilkinson were presented with silver watches, in recognition of their service that night and in the days that followed. Inscribed on each watch was the recipient's name and the following sentence:

'Presented for good work done when Zeppelin L33 was brought down in Essex Sept 24 1916'

In addition to the above, a silver watch was awarded posthumously to Alfred Wright, accepted by his father. Alfred Wright had died on November 13th from injuries sustained on the night the L33 came down. The 45 year old farmer owned Grove Farm, barely 300 yards from where the airship came to earth. He had witnessed the explosions and fire, so with his brother-in-law he had cautiously walked down Copt Hall Lane to investigate. Then, seeing the Germans walking towards them and fearing that they might be armed, they hurried back to the farm. Determined to alert the military authorities as soon as possible, Alfred Wright then sped off on his motorcycle towards West Mersea where he knew there was an Army post. Tragically while crossing the Strood, he collided with a car coming in the opposite direction, throwing him off his bike and badly injuring his leg. He had failed to see the car as it was driving without lights, as was the custom when Zeppelins were known to be active. It was also a moonless night with some patchy mist. The car was being driven by George Ernest Tiffin, a master butcher based in Brixton who was staying at his holiday home on Mersea. Tiffin was probably wary of using his car's headlights as eight days previously his wife had been fined £2 for not maintaining an adequate blackout at their West Mersea house. According to evidence given at Alfred Wright's inquest, Mr Tiffin had watched the Zeppelin fly over and soon afterwards had seen the glow from the subsequent fire. He had then set off in his car to investigate taking with him wife Florence and W Mussett (possibly the author's grandfather). On the way they picked up Sgt Baker of the military police. Whilst crossing the Strood they first heard and then briefly saw a motorcycle coming towards them in the centre of the road. They swerved to the left but were unable to prevent the motorcycle from striking the front wing of the car, knocking Mr Wright off his bike and onto the side of the road. He was taken back to his home and Dr J H Salter was summoned from Tolleshunt D'Arcy, five miles distant. Quickly realising that further urgent medical attention was needed, Dr Salter took the patient in his own car to Colchester Hospital where he was admitted. Alfred Wright's leg was amputated but his injuries failed to heal and gangrene set in, which resulted in his death seven weeks later. He was buried in the churchyard of St Nicholas Church, Little Wigborough, barely 600 yards from where the L33 fell. When his funeral took place later in November some of the remains of the Zeppelin, still strewn across Copt Hall Lane, had to be cut away to allow the hearse and mourners to approach the church. At the funeral service the Rector of Peldon, E G Bowring, himself also a Special Constable, said in his address that Alfred Wright had died for his country just as much as a man in the front line of battle. Amongst the many floral wreaths was one from the Special Constables and Police inscribed 'A tribute to his unselfish devotion'.

Wearing arm bands the special constables who captured the German crew.
From left to right: Charlie King, Edgar Nicholas, and Clement Hyam.
To the left of Clement Hyam is Edgar Dansie who managed the shop
The little girl to the left of the picture wearing a white dress is Marjorie Hyam, Clem Hyam's daughter.
Marjorie lived to the age of 103.

Another photograph of the Special Constables
From left to right:
Edgar Nicholas, unknown, Reverend Baring, Elisha Taylor, unknown, Charlie King, Tom Wyncoll, Clem Hyam

The two photographs above show how close L33 came to destroying New Hall Cottages

A photograph from inside the Zeppelin looking towards the nose

Dismantling one of the gondolas

Lord French visiting the Choat family

The narrow walkway that ran along the length of the L33 which the crew had to traverse to access the various manned stations inside the envelope and the external gondolas

The platform from which a member of the L33's crew would protect the Zeppelin's tail with a machine gun, now absent from its mounting

One of six propellers that drove the L33 through the air to a maximum speed of 28.7 m/s (64.2 mph)

The nose section propped with supports to allow precise measurements to be made

Inspecting the centre starboard side engine gondola

The crumpled tail section

The nose section. Clearly visible is the tube allowing access from the walkway to the gun platform on the front upper surface of the Zeppelin

An aerial view of the wreckage of the L33

The Lewis family pose beside their home, with the L33 barely 25 metres away

Chapter 4

As Böcker and his crew reached the Mersea end of the Strood under the watchful eyes of their armed escort they were met by West Mersea's vicar, the Reverend Charles Pierrepont Edwards, who having been awoken by the booming explosions from beyond the Strood channel, had set off on his bicycle to investigate. That Edwards should set off alone in the small hours when rumours were rife that Germans were about was not out of character for the clergyman known as 'The Fighting Parson'. Edwards, who was to serve as West Mersea's vicar for 48 years, earned his sobriquet when curate at St Saviour's Church in the borough of Southwark. There he had acquired a reputation for being able to physically restrain drunken or unruly parishioners, and if deemed necessary to use his fists to break up a fight. He was held in such esteem by the Southwark Police Division for his muscular presence that, when he left the parish for West Mersea, they presented him with a solid silver tea and coffee service, "in recognition of the service rendered them in the performance of their duties". Fiercely patriotic, Edwards served in the Essex Yeomanry during the Boer War. At the outbreak of the First World War he was attached as a Chaplain 4th class to the Suffolk Regiment, with whom he saw action during the ill-fated Gallipoli campaign. On 15th August 1915, just a week after landing on the peninsula, Edwards led a volunteer stretcher party, which despite being under heavy fire, succeeded in retrieving a number of wounded men from the battlefield. At one point, a stretcher bearer was hit in the waist by shrapnel immediately in front of him. Without hesitation, Edwards got the wounded man onto the stretcher and with the assistance of another stretcher bearer got him back behind the line. The two men then continued for some time to assist with the evacuation of the wounded. For his actions that day, the Chaplain was awarded the Military Cross.

In the absence of transport to deliver Böcker and his crew to the garrison town of Colchester, some eight miles distant, a suitable place to confine the Germans for the remainder of the night needed to be found. There was an Army tented encampment available between Beach Road and Lower Kingsland Road, but as this lacked adequate security, the vicar offered the use of the Parish Hall, behind the vicarage, Saint Peter's Cottage, number 8 High Street North, at which the exhausted Germans finally arrived at around 04.00. Despite the earliness of the hour, as news quickly spread around the island, then with a population of around two thousand, a crowd of curious, and in some cases distinctly hostile residents soon gathered outside the vicarage. A number expressed their anger that the 'baby killers', as Zeppelin crews were labelled by the newspapers, should be allowed the use of their Church Hall. In order to assuage these feelings, the vicar had the Union Flag raised and led a chorus of three cheers for the King as the Germans filed into the hall. While a few soldiers remained to stand guard over their prisoners, the vicar's wife Nancy, a prominent member of the local Voluntary Aid Detachment, tended to their welfare. Enlisting the help of two nurses and a couple of cooks, some refreshments and first aid was provided. A number of the crew needed attention for burns, and several had badly lacerated hands and fingers from clambering through the maze of sharp edged girders in their doomed attempt to keep their airship airborne. The most badly injured crewman, 31 year old Arthur Piepkorn, clearly in pain from his injuries sustained when he had leapt clear as the Zeppelin crashed, had his wounds treated at the Post Office at 11 High Street and was then offered a bed in a spare bedroom of St Peter's Cottage. Whilst the crew members gratefully accepted the hospitality that was offered, Captain Böcker remained aloof, declining any refreshments and refusing the offer of separate accommodation from his men in the form of a bed behind a screen in the Mission room.

With it being a Sunday, a sizeable crowd had gathered by the time that Captain Böcker and his crew were filed out of the Church Hall and onto the Army transport, which had arrived from the Colchester Garrison shortly before 09.00. Arthur Piepkorn was delivered to Colchester Hospital for further treatment for his injuries and the two officers, Captain Böcker and his second in command, the 23 year old executive officer, Leutnant Ernst Wilhelm Schiriltz, were sent to the Garrison's detention barracks for initial questioning. The remaining 18 crew were driven to the Colchester barracks in a separate lorry, arriving at 11.30. After a brief period of detention in Colchester, during which time there were some preliminary interrogations, the entire crew together with their captain were taken to London, where over a ten day period they were subjected to lengthy interrogation by a team of Intelligence officers led by Major Bernard Trench RM, head of the German Section of British Naval Intelligence. Trench was a fluent German speaker, having acquired his mastery of the language whilst serving 22 months of a four year prison sentence at Glatz in Silesia. In May 1910, when attached to the Naval Intelligence Division he had been arrested, together with his companion Captain Vivian Brandon, on the island of Borkum while studying the coastal defences. In December they were both convicted of espionage but Trench, together with another British subject caught spying, Captain Bertrand Stewart, were released early. They were pardoned by Kaiser Wilhelm as a gift to Ernst Augustus, Duke of Brunswick on his marriage to the Kaiser's daughter, Princess Victoria Louise of Prussia. Whilst serving his sentence in Silesia, Trench gained a considerable amount of information about German airship development from a fellow prisoner, the French intelligence officer Captain Luz, who had been caught spying on the Zeppelin airship works at Friedrichshafen.

During the period of interrogation, it became apparent that many of the German airmen were happy to be in the hands of British Intelligence, as they expected to be treated well. They were, however wary of the British public, as they had heard rumours of possible retribution. With the noted exception of Böcker and Schiriltz, a number of the crew were quite open with information. Trench was able to elicit this by claiming that British Naval intelligence already had a comprehensive knowledge of Zeppelin operations. Both officers and possibly other members of the crew were shown drawings of the latest Zeppelin designs, and Trench claimed to have spent a day at Friedrichshafen some weeks previously. Another tactic that Trench and his fellow interrogators employed was to ridicule the crew if they attempted to lie. Then, when pressed to justify the lie, further useful intelligence might unwittingly be revealed. Böcker and Schiriltz were shown photographs of the damage inflicted on Hull by Zeppelin L14 in a raid seven months earlier, in which both officers had participated. A number of the images were graphic depictions of corpses, including dead children. Trench then accused the two officers of murder and threatened them with a civil trial. Despite the threat Böcker gave little away. Schiriltz claimed that he had never lost his bearings over England, and such was his prowess with the bomb site and bomb aiming, that he had never dropped any bombs indiscriminately. However after more rigorous cross examination, Schiriltz did concede that navigational errors may have been made, and when pressed on the ethics of bombing of civilians he maintained that he had proudly carried out his duties and did not regret any of his actions. Major Trench's threat of a murder trial was a serious one, although once it was deemed that no further useful intelligence could be obtained the matter was dropped. The interrogations over, Böcker and Schiriltz were transferred to the German Officers' PoW camp at Donington Hall in Leicestershire and the remainder of the crew to Stobs PoW camp near Hawick, Scotland. Of the two officers only Ernst Schiriltz remained in captivity for the duration of the war, eventually being repatriated to Germany in November 1919. His captain however, as part of a prisoner exchange scheme, was returned to his homeland before hostilities ceased, on the customary condition that he would not serve in a combat role. Despite this stipulation, his days as an airship captain were not yet over. In June 1918 he was back at Nordholz, in command of his former airship L14, in his final wartime posting as Director of Training.

Ernst Schiriltz also served in the German Navy throughout the Second World War, reaching the rank of Vice Admiral, and was awarded the Knight's Cross of the Iron Cross in March 1945 in recognition of his service as Commander of the Atlantic Coast and of Fortress La Rochelle. He surrendered at the end of World War Two after the Allied siege of Fortress La Rochelle and shortly afterwards was acquitted of alleged war crimes. Schiriltz died in November 1978 at the age of 85.

Two of the 19 crew members who were incarcerated at Stobs camp, surrounded by the bleak moorland of the Scottish borders, nearly made it back to their homeland, by means of an audacious escape attempt. Max Emmerich and Wilhelm Jensen, together with four submariners, escaped from the camp on 22 August 1917 and after almost two weeks of stealthily making their way westward over the moors, evading British patrols, they reached the North Sea coast just south of Amble, where, by some means they managed to buy provisions. Making their way southward for another eight miles they reached the village of Cresswell where they seized a boat and immediately set out to sea. Fashioning a makeshift sail from their greatcoats they managed to avoid fishing boats and destroyers for three days until eventually, having sailed 170 miles from the Northumberland coast, they were spotted by the crew of a trawler who alerted the Navy. A passing destroyer then picked them up, bringing to an end their nearly three weeks of freedom. By the prisoners' own reckoning, after another twenty-four hours at sea they would have been safely home in Germany.

Chapter 5

By the time that the sun was beginning to rise over the carcase of the L33 on that memorable Sunday morning, a contingent of over 400 men of the 2nd/9th Manchester Division and 66th East Lancashire Division Cyclists from the Colchester Garrison were busy securing the site to deter any souvenir hunters among the ever-growing numbers of sightseers. However, despite their efforts and those of the special constables who had preceded them, several items and sections of framework were spirited away by some of the local farmworkers who arrived shortly after the Germans had left. A number of workers from Keston's Farm, just half a mile away across the fields to the north-west had already removed various items from the control gondola, including a brass instrument casing which together with a substantial length of girder was wrapped in a tarpaulin and hidden in the farmhouse pond. Concern that further items of significant intelligence value might be stripped from the largely intact Zeppelin hastened the Army to set up a closely guarded cordon. Once in place, none of the civilian onlookers who came in increasing numbers were able to encroach any closer than 200 yards. Despite this cordon, it soon became clear to the officers of the Intelligence Corps who arrived in the early afternoon, that several items had already been removed. As a consequence, later that same day soldiers with loudhailers rode around the nearby villages, ordering residents to return any booty to the military. Their exhortations met with mixed success, as a number of court cases held in the following weeks testify. The possession of any item from a hostile aircraft was in contravention of section 35B of the draconian 1914 Defence of the Realm Act and could incur heavy fines or worse. However, this did not prevent a number of nearby residents from hanging on to their 'trophies'. Perhaps unsurprisingly, given that the wreck was on their doorstep, the heads of household of the two New Hall Cottages were visited a few months later by the police, possibly following a tip off. Frederick Choat was initially found to be in possession of just a few metal fragments whilst his neighbour, Thomas Lewis, had amassed a considerable hoard of girders, other sections of duralumin and a measuring gauge, presumably from one of the gondolas. Lewis claimed that his 13 year old son Albert had found the gauge behind a hedge some weeks after the wreck had been removed, but due to it showing no evidence of having been exposed to the weather the police were unconvinced. Both Lewis and Choat were summoned to court on 31 March where the case against Lewis was dismissed on the grounds that he had 'acted in ignorance'. Choat was not so fortunate, receiving a caution. Before leaving the court Lewis had the temerity to ask the bench whether he could keep the items! Needless to say his request was denied. Perhaps the magistrate's leniency towards both men was in recognition of the trauma that the occupants of New Hall Cottages had been through on that fateful night. The case against Choat and Lewis was just one of several prosecutions held in the weeks and months that followed the downing of the L33. The newspapers of the time report several instances of fines given to individuals seeking to profit from selling pieces of duralumin to those who were eager to possess a souvenir of the historic event.

During the days that followed the downing of the L33, tens of thousands of sightseers came to view the downed leviathan, some tramping across fields of crops yet to be harvested. When eventually arriving at the wreckage, many were no doubt disappointed that armed sentries prevented them from approaching any closer than 200 yards. The services of the Special Constables were once again employed, this time under the direction of Captain Ffinch, to manage the flow of traffic that clogged the narrow lanes. Edward Hutley, the owner of Brick House Farm at Great Wigborough, in an attempt to protect what remained of his eight acres of crops, cut down a hedge and built a gate where one of his labourers, Harold Ponder, was stationed to collect tuppence from all who passed through. Such was the demand to see the Zeppelin that in just over a week nearly £80 was collected which Farmer Hutley donated to a number of war charities including the Red Cross. In the weeks before the remains of the Zeppelin were broken up and carried away, it has been estimated that something in the order of 250,000 visitors came to visit the wreck of what had until very recently been the pride of the Imperial German Navy Airship Division. It was not only local residents who were drawn to the remains of the L33. Sir John French, Commander in Chief of the British Home Forces, Sir William Robertson, Chief of the Imperial General Staff and Commodore Murray F Sueter, Director of the Air Department and Officer Commanding the Royal Naval Air Service were the most notable of a considerable number of senior military personnel who came to inspect the site. During their visit Sir John's and his entourage spent some chatting with the Choat and Lewis families about their narrow escape when the L33 landed on their doorsteps. The Secretary of State for War, David Lloyd George, and the First Lord of the Admiralty, Arthur Balfour, perhaps with foreknowledge that their tour of the site was to be caught on camera by Gaumont, also made the journey to north Essex. Other notable visitors were the two RFC pilots Lt Frederic Sowrey, and his friend and fellow officer of 39 Squadron, Lt Leefe Robinson VC, by then household names due to their exploits in bringing about the destruction of the L32 (see below) and SL-11. A visit to the Zeppelin clearly left a lasting impression on many who visited the site. One of those visitors was 40 year old schoolmistress Rose Luard who travelled the five or so miles from Birch to join the throng of sightseers on that first Sunday. Later that day she wrote a long letter to her older sister Kate describing her impressions of the day.

'The Zep. is a vast monster, lying in its naked framework of girders, across 2 fields & the land between them. Parts of it look absolutely unhurt, but of course the gas bag is all burnt and the bottom machinery part is all smashed on the ground, & its back is broken & bent in several places, so that it looks like a gigantic antediluvian reptile of sorts, with its nose posed in the air, & its tail intact behind. I tried to make a very rough sketch of its shape as it looked from the stubble field, which was the nearest we were allowed to go, about a field off. It was something like the overleaf (referring to her sketch that accompanied the letter) *but of course all the papers will have lovely photographs of it I expect. No one was allowed to go nearer than a field off: it was being guarded by a cordon of soldiers so one couldn't see any details of where the guns had been or the propeller or anything. But the mere sight of the huge reptile, all gleaming girders in the bright sun was extraordinarily thrilling. And our aeroplanes were brightly buzzing in the blue sky over head. A dazzling day & a very happy heterogeneous crowd of country people, mixed with Colchester of course, all taking their Sunday matins in that pleasant form. A good many soldiers and officers of course from Colchester, with their womenfolk & I saw one old General & lots of red tabs prancing about on the stubble with the common herd. It was Fred & I who swelled the godless crowd. I persuaded him to come with me in the morning. Daisy & Nettie have gone this afternoon, but I expect the few hundreds will have swelled to thousands this afternoon. It was such a jolly local crowd, gazing at their own Zeppelin, none of your hoards from London. Our Policemen got near & picked up a bit of the burnt gas bag covering and gave it to George whom I met on the field & he gave a bit to me. It is very fine canvas with a silky sheen on it. I can't tell you how jolly it felt to look & know that our beloved little sea creek corner of Essex has at last come into its own in the Zeppelin line, after having impotently heard them come & go all this long time & Little Wigborough of all places!'*

Police Constable Albert Lintott (stationed at Birch) giving a sense of scale by posing beside one of the L33's propellors

A 1/72 scale model (built by the author) of a Be2c fighter of type used by 2nd Lt de Bathe Brandon in his attack on L33 (this particular model is of the aircraft No 2693 piloted by Lt William Leefe Robinson VC in the shooting down of SL 11)

It was not only in that usually quiet corner of North East Essex where crowds were gathering in their thousands to inspect the burnt out remains of what had been one of the Imperial German Navy's most advanced airships. Around the same time that the L33 was preparing to crash land over the marshes bordering the Strood Channel, some 35 miles away Second Lieutenant Frederick Sowery was training his gunsights on the L32 as he approached the huge airship from below. Opening fire, his bullets raked along the length of the Zeppelin seemingly with no effect until eventually, rounds from Sowery's third drum of ammunition started a fire which spread rapidly, engulfing the whole airship. The Zeppelin plunged to earth at Snail's Hall farm, Great Burstead, just to the south of Billericay, killing all 22 on board. The fiery spectacle of the immolation of the L32, was witnessed, as had been the case with the destruction of the SL 11 just three weeks earlier, by thousands of Londoners and residents of the Essex and Kent. By Sunday morning thousands of onlookers had gathered to view the barely recognisable tangled mass of blackened wire and girders.

The two wrecked Zeppelins that now lay in Essex fields provided the British authorities with a treasure trove of intelligence. Of the two Zeppelins, the L33, being largely intact was the greater prize, although found in the control gondola of the L32 was a charred but still largely legible copy of the newly issued German Navy signal book. This was swiftly passed on to the Admiralty code breakers leaving the German Navy unaware for some time that their codes had been compromised. However, the L33 was the main focus for the intelligence gatherers. From the first day of its fortuitous arrival until its final dismantlement and removal in late February 1917, the Zeppelin was examined minutely by technicians and draughtsmen, under the direction of The Admiralty. They measured and photographed every conceivable detail, in order to gain the best possible understanding of the construction and operation of the airship. To assist the technicians in their task, on 2 October, three members of L33's crew were escorted back to the crash site from where they were temporarily being held prisoner in London, to explain the workings of certain items of the Zeppelin's equipment. The intelligence gathered at Little Wigborough, together with information extracted by the Admiralty's inquisitors from the captured crews of L7, L15, and the L33, revealed a comprehensive insight into the strategy, tactics and capabilities (and deficiencies) of the German Naval Airship Division. The lessons learned enabled the British Home forces to hone their anti-Zeppelin strategies in the battle to defend Britain from strategic bombing, a battle that was increasingly tipping in Britain's favour. The loss of two of Germany's most modern airships in one night represented a major victory for Britain's home defence forces and a shattering blow to Germany's Naval Airship Division. As far as Britain's ability to defend itself from aerial bombardment by airships was concerned, the tide had truly turned. The advantage now lay with the defenders.

Part 2

Chapter 1

Despite the loss of the two of its most advanced Zeppelins in a single raid, the German Naval Airship Division persisted with the strategic bombing campaign. The very next day, on September 25, nine Zeppelins were launched to attack targets in Britain. As on the previous raid, the older and more vulnerable airships targeted the less well defended Midlands and only the more capable L30 and L31 were ordered to once again attack London. All of the Zeppelins returned safely to their bases, although damage caused was minimal and neither of the L30s managed to reach London due to unfavourable weather.

Determined to inflict serious damage on Britain's capital, Strasser next sent out his airships on October 1, when eleven were launched into the deteriorating autumnal weather. Only L31, captained by the Imperial German Navy's most successful airship Captain, Heinrich Mathy, attempted to attack London. Approaching the capital from the north, Mathy was confronted by a formidable barrage of anti-aircraft fire. A further threat to the Zeppelin were four BE2c fighters, that despite the shells bursting nearby closed in on their target. The first pilot to come within range was Second Lieutenant Wulstan Joseph Tempest who engaged his prey at just about the limit of his aircraft's flight ceiling.

"As I drew up to the Zeppelin, to my relief I found the nearest shells were bursting quite three miles away. The Zeppelin was now nearly 15,000 feet high and climbing rapidly. I therefore decided to dive at her, for though I held a slight advantage in speed, she was climbing like a rocket and leaving me standing. I accordingly gave a tremendous pump at my petrol tank, and dived straight at her, firing a burst straight into her as I came. I let her have another burst as I passed under her tail, and flying along underneath her, pumped lead into her for all I was worth. I could see tracer bullets flying from her in all directions, but I was too close under her for her to concentrate on me. As I was firing, I noticed her begin to go red inside like an enormous Chinese lantern and then a flame shoot out on the front part of her and I realised she was on fire. She then shot up about 200 feet, paused, and came roaring down straight on to me before I had time to get out of the way. I nose-dived for all I was worth, with the Zepp tearing after me, and expected every minute to be engulfed in the flames. I put my machine into a spin and just managed to corkscrew out of the way as she shot past me, roaring like a furnace."

The burning wreckage of L31 plummeted to earth in a field at Oakmere Farm, outside Potters Bar. All twenty-one on board were killed. The body of the Zeppelin's captain Heinrich Mathy was found some distance from the wreckage having jumped clear of the conflagration as the ship fell. The loss of an airship commander of such legendary status was a major blow to the morale of the men of the Naval Airship Division. One petty officer wrote, somewhat presciently:

"There was only one airship commander with whom I ever flew that I would have trusted to find his way over England without making a bad mistake. The was Heinrich Mathy…It was the aeroplane firing the incendiary bullet that brought about his downfall and with him the life and soul of our airship service went out too."

After the destruction of the L31, so soon after the loss of both the L32 and L33 together with their experienced crews, it became abundantly clear to Strasser that the chances of a Zeppelin breaching London's defences and returning home safely were becoming increasingly slim. As a consequence, when the next raids against England were mounted, on November 27, the capital was avoided, and the targets selected were in the Midlands and on Tyneside. The raid proved to be a disaster for The Naval Airship Division with two Zeppelins shot down in flames by fighters. The L34 was destroyed off the coast near the mouth of the river Tees, and the L21 which was attacked by three fighters came down into the sea about ten miles east of Lowestoft. Once more all on board both airships perished. There were no further raids launched in 1916, although two more Zeppelins were lost through accidents on December 28. Caught by a powerful gust as she was being walked into her shed at Tondern, the L24 broke her back and caught fire. The fire spread to L17, already in the double hanger, resulting in the total loss of both airships.

With losses mounting to unsustainable levels Strasser had to argue his case most forcibly with Fleet Command to prevent the complete abandonment of the bombing campaign. There was a general acceptance within the Naval Airship Division that in order to continue bombing operations without further crippling losses the Zeppelins would need to climb to greater altitudes, where they would present a smaller target for the anti-aircraft artillery and be beyond the maximum ceiling of defending fighters. To achieve this end, all future military Zeppelins built incorporated modifications, both to reduce their weight and increase their lift. To reduce the weight of the 'Height Climbers', as the next generation of Zeppelins were known, one of the six engines was removed and the Zeppelin's structure was lightened, albeit at the expense of its strength. Gas cell weight was reduced by using only two layers of gold beaters' skin rather than three, and eventually silk fabric was used instead of cotton. The total volume of the gas cells was increased to provide greater lift. With all these modifications the Zeppelins were able to operate over England at altitudes between 16,000 and 20,000 feet, beyond the reach of most of the anti-aircraft guns and the British Home Defence Force's fighters. Operating in the stratosphere caused other problems though. The lower levels of oxygen reduced the power output of the engines by up to 50%, giving a maximum speed of only 45 m.p.h. at 20,000 feet compared to 62 m.p.h. at sea level. The thin air could also induce altitude sickness, requiring the crew to breath from oxygen bottles. There was also the intense cold, which caused numerous cases of frostbite in the unheated Zeppelins. For the German meteorologists, hampered by a lack of any weather station West of Bruges, predicting the wind strength or direction in the stratosphere proved nigh on impossible, and on many occasions during subsequent operations, airships were imperilled by extreme winds in the upper atmosphere that had not been forecast. Being above all but the highest cirrus clouds, navigating by observing landmarks proved challenging and under the influence of the unforeseen Jetstream a Zeppelin could soon become hopelessly lost. At night, with a thick blanket of cloud beneath him and at the mercy of much stronger winds than predicted, an airship commander became increasingly reliant on taking radio bearings. However, as the system used required the Zeppelin to send out a signal to ashore station the airship's position could also be determined by the British radio monitoring stations who would then alert the Home Defence Forces.

The first raids by the new "height climbers" took place on March 16, 1917, when five Zeppelins were ordered to attack London. Again, the operation was a failure, although it was the weather rather than the actions of the defending forces that was responsible. Unbeknownst to both the crews and the German weather forecasters, a deepening low-pressure system with associated storm force winds was approaching from the north-west. Battling against the opposing winds the Zeppelins only just managed reach the British coast and drop a few bombs over the Kent countryside, causing minimal damage. Then at the mercy of the fierce winds the airships were driven South over the channel and into France. As dawn was breaking, L39 drifted over Compiegne where French anti-aircraft guns opened up, firing in excess of one hundred shells over a fifteen-minute interval. Eventually one of the shells struck the Zeppelin amidships causing her to break into two sections which then fell to earth in flames. The remaining four airships, after highly eventful flights of over twenty-four hours duration, finally returned safely to bases in Belgium and Germany, although L35 was badly damaged on entering her hanger.

The next raid took place on May 23, three days after the new moon, when six Zeppelins were ordered to attack London. Only L43 claimed to have dropped bombs on the capital, although British authorities tracked the airship over Suffolk and Norfolk. L42 scattered a few bombs harmlessly between Mildenhall and Dereham whilst the crew thought they were over Sheerness. L44, with Strasser on board, was fortunate to return safely after a catalogue of technical problems and equipment failures. The three remaining Zeppelins, flying high above a solid blanket of cloud with only the vaguest idea as to their position, succeeded only in dropping three of their bombs on land. British records show that the raid caused damage worth £599, and that one man was killed. Once again, the deteriorating weather and the difficulties in operating at extreme altitudes resulted in the raid being ineffectual. Despite the continuing poor returns, Strasser remained convinced as to the value of such raids to the German war effort. However, amongst the German High Command there were serious doubts. Commenting on the Naval Staff's unduly optimistic report on the latest raids Kaiser Wilhelm noted:

"In spite of this success, I am of the opinion that the day of the airship is past for attacks on London. They should be used as scouts for the High Seas Fleet, and for strategic reconnaissance, not for bombing raids on London."

The Chief of the Naval Staff came to Strasser's defence and argued that large numbers of troops, guns and aeroplanes would be released for the Western Front if the airships were to cease their attacks. Presented with this argument the Kaiser acquiesced and the raids continued.

However, a further shattering blow to the fortunes of the Airship Division occurred on the next raid. This was mounted on June 16, to coincide with the following new moon on June 19. Being so close to the summer solstice and operating at high altitude the Zeppelins would have been clearly visible for all but three to four hours of semi darkness. Against the better judgement of a number of his junior officers Strasser, still asserting that his "height climbers" were immune from attack by fighters, sent out six Zeppelins to attack London. Events were to prove him wrong, with fatal consequences for the crew of L48. Only two ships succeeded in reaching England, L46 and L47 being unable to leave their sheds due to cross winds, and L44 and L45 both turning back following engine failures. L42 was prevented from reaching London but despite this setback managed to drop bombs on Ramsgate, striking a naval ammunition depot, causing three fatalities and sixteen injured, two of them servicemen. L48's progress was severely slowed by engine problems and a frozen compass made navigation difficult. Being too late to reach London, the commander, Franz Eichler, accompanied by Strasser's deputy Vicktor Schultz, decided to bomb the Naval dockyard at Harwich and then steer for home before dawn broke. L48 crossed the English coast near Shingle Street and then turned south to approach the target from the north. From an altitude of over 18,000 feet at around 03.00 the crew released their bombs on what they thought was the Naval dockyard. However, such was the rudimentary nature of the science of bomb aiming, with any errors magnified by the extreme altitude, that despite clear visibility above the target, the bombs fell in fields five miles to the north. In the midsummer twilight, the black painted underside of the Zeppelin did little to conceal the airship from the gunners below, provoking a formidable barrage of anti-aircraft fire from both land-based guns and warships. But the shells were unable to reach their target, exploding harmlessly below. Having delivered their bombs and cleared the area, the crew reduced altitude to 13,000 feet and steered for home, although the frozen compass resulted in them taking a more northerly course, keeping them over the Suffolk countryside rather than out over the sea. Unbeknownst to the crew, in hot pursuit were 2nd Lt L.P. Watkins flying in a BE 12 fighter aircraft and Captain R.H.M.S. Saundby in a DH2, just two of a number of Home Defence force pilots who were in the air that night. Both pilots succeeded in intercepting the Zeppelin and saw their machine gun rounds strike home - although it was Watkins who was to receive the greater credit for the destruction of the Zeppelin.

Coaxing his aircraft up to its maximum ceiling of over 13,000 feet Watkins was able to bring the airship within range. Whilst still 500 feet below the Zeppelin and on his third drum of ammunition, Watkins observed his rounds starting a fire at the tail which soon engulfed the entire airship. The flaming L48 fell to earth in a field at Holly Tree Farm, near Theberton, although more slowly than had been the case with either the L31 or L32. As a consequence of this more gradual descent three of the crew survived their ordeal. Heinrich Ellerkamm escaped with only minor burns and Executive Officer Otto Mieth survived with two broken legs, although the more seriously injured Wilhelm Uecker never fully recovered from his wounds, dying on Armistice Day 1918.

No further Zeppelin losses were incurred when eight airships next attacked targets in the north of England on 21/22 August, 1917. Strasser accompanied the raid aboard L46. Once again, very little was achieved, the few bombs dropped mostly falling harmlessly. The only casualty of the raid was one of the pilots of the pursuing aircraft, Lt J A Dales, who crashed his BE 2c fighter on landing. A total of nineteen aircraft took off in pursuit of the raiders but were unable to climb to a sufficient altitude to mount an attack. Operating at altitudes approaching 20,000 feet, whilst invulnerable to either attack by fighters or from ground fire, presented the Zeppelin crews with significant obstacles to accurate navigation and bomb aiming. In the intense cold, compasses froze, and oxygen-starved engines lacked power. Breathing the thin air, despite the support of compressed oxygen equipment, severely impaired the crew's ability to carry out their duties.

The last significant raid of 1917 against targets in England, on October 19/20, came to be known as the 'silent raid', due in part to the high-altitude approach of the Zeppelins dampening the engine noise. Also, given that the airships were beyond the anti-aircraft gun's range, the British guns were ordered to remain muzzled, lest they should betray their position and help guide the enemy to its targets. After the raid there was some speculation that the Zeppelins had cut their engines and allowed the wind to drift them towards the target. This was not possible however, as due to the extreme cold at such altitudes, a shutdown engine would have soon frozen solid and become impossible to re-start. A total of eleven airships took part in the raid, although only seven would return. The targets chosen by Strasser were the industrial regions of the north of England. The airships left their sheds around midday, their crews confident of success given the relatively benign weather forecast. As the airships broke free of their mooring ropes the crews had no way of knowing that a deepening depression over Iceland was sweeping south-east towards the British Isles, bringing northerly gale force winds. The last great Zeppelin raid of the First World War was heading for disaster.

As the Zeppelins made their way across the North Sea and climbed to above 16,000 feet the crews found conditions very different from what had been predicted by the meteorologists. As the airships battled against the freshening northerly wind, it became increasingly apparent that the intended targets would be beyond reach. With a mostly unbroken blanket of cloud beneath them and fierce winds driving them southwards, those bombs that were dropped generally fell harmlessly in the countryside. The greatest destruction was inflicted by Zeppelin L45, which more by chance than through skilful navigation, approached London from the north. Observing the unmistakable outline of the Thames through fleeting breaks in the clouds, the airship dropped three 660 lb bombs which fell in Piccadilly, Camberwell, and Hither Green respectively. In total thirty-three people were killed and fifty were injured.

On turning east to make its way back to Germany, the L45 was intercepted over the river Medway by 2nd Lt T. B. Pritchard, flying a BE 2c. Although 2,000 feet below the airship, Pritchard opened fire but was unable to follow his prey when the Zeppelin dropped ballast and rapidly rose several thousand feet. This manoeuvre, whilst evading the fighter, effectively sealed the Zeppelin's fate. As it was now exposed to the much fiercer northerly winds at a higher altitude, the airship was driven south at an alarming rate. Further technical problems exacerbated the crew's dire situation and eventually, with fuel nearly exhausted, the Zeppelin crash landed in France where the crew surrendered to some nearby French troops. A not dissimilar fate befell L49 and L50. The L49 crash landed, pretty much intact, in woodland on the slopes of the river Apance, near Bourbonne-les-Bains in north-east France, the crew of nineteen being taken prisoner. L50, with the crew hopelessly lost, with failing engines and with insufficient fuel to have any chance of making it back to Germany, was intentionally flown at speed into the ground east of Langres so as to render her unusable by the enemy. As the airship struck the ground, the control gondola broke away and sixteen of the twenty-man crew managed to jump clear. The now much lightened airship soared heavenwards again carrying the remaining four helpless crew members with her. The uncontrollable airship at the complete mercy of the wind continued to fly south over France as night fell. As no wreckage has ever been found it has been assumed that the airship eventually crashed and then sank in the Mediterranean. Also destined not to return was the ill-fated L44. Despite leaving her base at Ahlhorn at 13.00 hours, such was the effect of the head wind, that it was not until around 19.45 that she reached the English coast, east of the Wash. Driven south by the northerly gales the Zeppelin released bombs near Herne Bay, damaging an inn, before being traced crossing the coast between Dover and North Foreland around 21.50. It is possible that attempts by Captain Stabbert to follow a course home were thwarted by engine problems, in addition to the unfavourable weather, resulting in the airship appearing at 07.45 the following morning, perilously close to the Western Front, and in range of the French 75 mm anti-aircraft guns. On detecting enemy fire the Zeppelin rapidly soared from 12,000 to 19,000 feet but in vain. An incendiary round entered the hull and ignited the leaking hydrogen. Wreathed in flames, the doomed Zeppelin fell nose first, scattering wreckage near the town of Saint-Clement in Lorraine. All crew members perished.

With the loss of four airships and with minimal damage caused to the enemy, the raid was another hammer blow to the fortunes of the Imperial German Navy Airship Division. In his report on the raid to Admiral Scheer, Strasser primarily blamed the weather service for failing to obtain high altitude wind measurements from Ostend, the absence of such information ultimately leading to the catastrophe that followed. The disastrous outcome of the raid was hailed by the British press as perhaps the 'beginning of the end' of the Zeppelin menace, although under other circumstances things might have been very different. With more benign meteorological conditions the 'height climbers' would have been able to roam relatively unhindered over London, free to bomb at will. Given the Zeppelins' extreme altitude, the anti-aircraft guns and probing searchlights would have presented little threat, and, the defending fighter aircraft, unable to climb to such lofty heights, would have been powerless to trouble their prey. That night, not one of the seventy-three pilots who took to the air to counter the attack was able to engage the enemy, given the limited ceiling of their aircraft. With the freedom to operate unhindered over the city, the large force of Zeppelins could have inflicted considerable damage and loss of life. However, as has already been mentioned, with rudimentary navigation and bomb aiming, exacerbated by the difficulties of operating at extreme altitude and with crews often struggling with the effects of altitude sickness, a concentrated attack would have been out of the question.

Despite the crippling loss of four Zeppelins in a single raid, Strasser was still determined to take the fight to the British. His confidence was buoyed by the installation of the new Maybach "altitude motors" in the next generation of Zeppelins off the production line. Previous airships had all been fitted with the same motor since the beginning of the war, which, due to oxygen starvation at altitude, lost nearly half of its power. As a consequence, maximum speed fell from 62 mph to 45 mph, making forward progress against a typical headwind experienced in the upper atmosphere nigh on impossible. In addition to increased speed, the Zeppelins would in future benefit from two new radio sending stations at Tondern and Cleve, 250 miles to the south-south-west of the Rhineland. These stations transmitted directional signals at regular intervals, from which the Zeppelins could determine their position. Prior to this development, an airship had to send a signal to the ground stations to request bearings, in order to fix its position. The weakness of this method was that it betrayed a Zeppelin's position to the British, whose listening stations were constantly monitoring the radio frequencies that the German Airship Service used.

For the remainder of 1917 Strasser's plans to test his new, more capable Zeppelins against the defences of the British were frequently thwarted by deteriorating late autumn, and then winter weather. On December 18, during a break in the weather, five Zeppelins were launched on Strasser's orders to attack targets in the industrial north. Once again, the more benign conditions at ground level proved illusory. Strasser accompanied the attempted raid aboard L58, which despite being fitted with the new altitude motors, was unable to make any headway against the 45 mph headwinds encountered at 13,000 feet. All the remaining Zeppelins experienced similar difficulties and at 20.30 Strasser reluctantly ordered all commanders to return to their bases. The weather had beaten them once again.

Other than the occasional patrol over the German Bight the Airships remained in their sheds, secure from the winter storms which lasted into the New Year. On the late afternoon of Saturday January 5, 1918, with the airships still consigned to their sheds, the base at Ahlhorn was rocked by a series of explosions. In the space of a few short minutes five airships were reduced to a smouldering, tangled heap of wreckage. Following a thorough enquiry, possible causes of the catastrophe were identified. Petrol fumes either near or inside the gondola of L51 had been ignited, probably inadvertently by civilian contractors tasked with cleaning the gondola's flooring. Within moments L51 was engulfed in flames, the inferno soon spreading to the nearby L47 and L58 in sheds 1 and 2. The intense heat from the burning hydrogen was sufficient to bring about the destruction of L46 and the wooden-built SL 20 in sheds 3 and 4 half a mile distant. It is thought that the heat from the flames had expanded the hydrogen gas in the airships' gas cells causing the hydrogen to vent. The mixture of hydrogen and air filling the sheds had then exploded, destroying the two airships, and reducing the sheds to rubble. The human cost of the disaster was 10 servicemen killed and 134 injured, 30 of them seriously. In addition, 4 civilian workmen, who had been working on the SL30, were also killed. A total of 5 airships were reduced to smouldering wrecks and the Ahlhorn base was put out of action for four months. It is thought that Strasser never recovered from this shattering blow to the forces under his command. Although remaining bullish in public, privately he expressed his fears for the future of the Airship Service. In a private letter he wrote:

"It was terrible to see the proud Ahlhorn base collapse in wreckage before my eyes in the space of a minute. But we can overcome it. We have sheds and ships to fill the gap, and the determination is there to triumph over all difficulties with our heads held high."

With the German army stalled on the Western Front, the High Seas Fleet mostly confined to port and the German U Boat threat diminishing, Strasser possibly still considered that it could be the Imperial Airship Naval Division's contribution that would turn the war in Germany's favour and bring ultimate victory in 1918.

During the first few months of the New Year, whilst the German High Command were preparing the spring offensives to force the allies into a negotiated peace, Strasser continued to explore every opportunity to inflict damage to the British war effort through the Zeppelins' strategic bombing campaign. However, with the airships' vulnerability to the typical winter weather, it was not until March 12 that conditions were deemed adequate to launch the first bombing raids of the year. That afternoon, five of the newest Zeppelins, including the brand new L63 which had only been delivered to Nordholz two days previously, were released from their mooring ropes to set course for industrial targets in the midlands. Strasser led the way in L62. The weather was clear over the German Bight but on approaching the English coast the airships encountered a thick blanket of cloud below their altitude of around 16,000 to 18,000 feet. Nevertheless, they pressed on westwards, their position being determined in part by radio bearings. Bombs were released on what were believed to be industrial targets, but in most cases these fell harmlessly in fields, or in the North Sea. However, six bombs dropped by L63 did damage houses in Hull. L54 released her bombs over what was believed to be Grimsby but they fell among trawlers in the North Sea. Some of the trawlers fired back with small anti-aircraft weapons, despite the Zeppelin being well out of range. All the Zeppelins returned to their bases unscathed, although some holes were found in gas cell 9 of L54. Initially thought to be the result of enemy fire, on closer inspection the cause was found to be due to shards of ice thrown by the propellers of the midship gondolas, a not uncommon hazard when operating at extreme altitudes. L53 also suffered damage from a heavy landing at Nordholz, as the airship failed to respond to Captain Prolss' orders to reduce speed. The four crew members manning the two rear engines had been overcome with carbon monoxide poisoning from a cracked exhaust pipe for some hours and hence could not respond to the engine telegraph command to reduce power. Their fate remained undiscovered until L53 landed at Nordholz. Two of the crew were revived after being carried into the fresh air but the other two were pronounced dead. The service had suffered two fatalities, one more than in England as a result of the raid. The ineffectiveness of the raid was once more largely due to the weather and also the limitations of the rudimentary radio direction finding. Had the weather been more favourable the Zeppelins may well have inflicted far greater damage but would of course been much more vulnerable from the fighter aircraft that hunted and stalked their prey in ever increasing numbers.

Despite the minimal returns of the raid on March 12, Strasser ordered a further raid on the industrial midlands the next day. During the afternoon, three Zeppelins, L52, L56 and L42, gently lifted off from their mooring ropes and set course for England. Once again, the weather was to intervene, causing Strasser to recall the craft at 19.13, when as the wind was veering easterly and strengthening. However, only L52 and L56, cruising above the Frisian Islands when they received the message, obeyed the order. L42 was by then already just off the Northumberland coast and did not acknowledge Strasser's recall. Commander Kapitanleutnant Max Dietrich chose to delay complying with the order as an inviting target of a British convoy was in sight. Dietrich hoped to attack the convoy before returning to Nordholz but the English coast then came into sight view. The temptation to press on with the raid proved too great for Dietrich and his crew, so despite the risk to his career in the service, should his mission fail, Dietrich maintained course for England. As darkness fell, the twinkling lights of Hartlepool were clearly visible from L42's altitude of 16,400 feet. With his engines idling, Dietrich allowed the northerly wind to carry the nearly silent Zeppelin over West Hartlepool undetected. In all, twenty-one 50Kg bombs exploded in the town causing considerable damage, later valued at £14,280. Eight people were killed and twenty-nine were injured. The devastating attack took only ten minutes. As L42 steered for home she was engaged by the anti-aircraft defences but to no effect. The Zeppelin encountered the predicted head wind throughout her return flight to Nordholz and it was not until twelve hours after the attack that she landed without incident. Despite disobeying his commander's orders Dietrich only received a mild official rebuke from Strasser. According to Dietrich, after he had given his verbal report Strasser smiled and remarked, 'In honour of your successful attack, I name you "Count of Hartlepool."

It was not until a month later, on April 12, 1918, that a fleet of five of the newest Zeppelins left their sheds to bomb targets in the industrial midlands. Each of the airships was loaded with 3,000 Kg of bombs including four of 300 Kg. Despite the optimistic weather forecast, once over the North Sea the crews faced frequent rain squalls and an unbroken blanket of cloud, forcing them to rely solely on radio bearings for navigation. Bombing blind, with radio bearings and dead reckoning navigation as their only guide, L60, L63 and L64 between them claimed to have attacked Leeds, Grimsby and Hull, but of the bombs traced none fell on their intended targets. Both L63 and L64 had repeated engine failures and L64 suffered significant damage from a heavy landing at Nordholz keeping her unserviceable until 29 April. Much greater success however was achieved by Commander Hauptmann Kuno Manger and his crew in L62. Battling against the elements and poor visibility L62 was over land for six hours, as Manger sought suitable targets for his bombs. His primary objective was Birmingham, but despite releasing his entire bomb load of 2½ tonnes, no major damage or loss of life resulted except for an unfortunate bullock, heifer and lamb, killed at Baginton, close to what is now Coventry Airport. Manger claimed to have bombed Nottingham and an "unidentified city" although of those bombs which were traced, most fell harmlessly in open country, as was so often the case. Shortly after releasing the last of her bombs, L62 encountered Lt C.H. Noble-Campbell of No 38 Squadron flying an FE 2b. After a pursuit lasting half an hour Noble-Campbell gradually closed on the Zeppelin and then when in range opened fire with his Lewis machine gun, only to be met with accurate return fire from the mechanics in one of the airship's gondolas, wounding the Englishman and forcing him to break off his attack. Despite his wounds and the damage to his aircraft, he was able to land safely at Coventry. L62's journey home was not without further incident. Passing over Norfolk the Zeppelin was fired at by anti-aircraft guns at Pulham and Great Yarmouth, causing a significant loss of hydrogen due to one of the gas cells being punctured by shell fragments.

The Zeppelin that penetrated furthest into Great Britain's airspace that night was L61, commanded by Kapitanleutnant Herbert Ehrlich. Ehrlich's aim was to attack Sheffield, but he passed south of his intended target without seeing it, due to an effective blackout. By maintaining his course Ehrlich would have passed over the prize target of Liverpool, but over Runcorn, just ten miles short of Liverpool, unaware of his precise location Ehrlich turned north and, on seeing the reddish glow of blast furnaces, released most of his bomb load on a target he believed to be Sheffield. In reality L61 had bombed Wigan and the surrounding area, killing five individuals of whom three were children, and injuring twelve. The damage caused by the raid was valued at over £11,000. The bulk of her bomb load gone, L61 made her way back towards the coast, dropping her last four remaining 300kg bombs in fields near the village of Aspull where the blast caused significant damage to some nearby cottages. Her mission completed, L61 crossed the coast by the mouth of the Humber where she came under fire from guns at Kilnsea on the Spurn peninsula and from HMS Albion, but without result. Flying over the North Sea at a reduced altitude of 6,500 feet to lessen the headwind, L61 was spotted by a patrolling F.2a flying boat, at a distance of around ten miles. With the limited speed advantage that the aeroplane had over the Zeppelin, together with a much inferior flight ceiling, an interception proved impossible, as the airship soared to over 22,000 feet and disappeared from view. Despite experiencing a number of engine failures - at one stage only the port engine in the rear gondola was running - L61 eventually landed at Wittmundhaven, having been airborne for nearly twenty-one hours.

Throughout the remainder of the spring and early summer of 1918, as the German offensive on the Western Front faltered, no further bombing raids by Imperial German airships were attempted. The service remained operationally active however, engaged in scouting missions over the North Sea in support of the High Seas Fleet. No losses to British aircraft occurred during this period, as the heavy twin-engined F.2a flying boats employed to patrol the North Sea had neither the speed nor ceiling to threaten the Zeppelins, which warily kept at higher altitudes. During one of the scouting missions, L62 was lost with all hands although not as a result of enemy action. On May 10, flying at around 1,000 feet a few miles to the north-west of Heligoland, L62 was seen to disappear into a towering cumulonimbus cloud. Very shortly afterwards a loud explosion was heard and flaming sections of the destroyed airship fell into the sea, some landing on the trawler Bergedorf, whose crew were the only witnesses of L62's demise. There were no survivors and only five bodies from the crew of twenty were recovered. The explanation for L62's loss remains unknown, a possible cause being an electrical discharge in the storm cloud detonating the bomb load.

Once the Admiralty became aware of L62's loss, they attributed its destruction to the actions of the crew of an F.2a flying boat, which had reported attacking a Zeppelin not far from where L62 was lost. According to Captain A H Munday's report of the encounter, the crew had observed their explosive machine gun rounds striking the airship in the area of the port engine, causing the Zeppelin to sharply turn to port. Through releasing water ballast the airship was then seen to climb out of range, leaving a trail of smoke. However, research by the author Douglas H Robinson in the German archives has determined that the Zeppelin attacked by the flying boat was not L62, but L56. After the encounter L56 returned to her base undamaged, having been out of range of the flying boat's fire throughout the attack, contrary to Captain Munday's report. The swirling cloud of exploding and flaming tracer rounds in the line of sight of the Zeppelin, although falling short, could, in the heat of battle have convinced Munday and his crew that the target had been struck.

With the Zeppelins now only making rare forays into Britain's air space and with the RAF's twin engined flying boats struggling to reach the altitude of the Zeppelins that patrolled the North Sea, the opportunities for the British forces to inflict further losses on the remaining airships were becoming increasingly rare. As a consequence the Admiralty decided to take the attack to the Germans and to attempt to destroy the Zeppelins at their home bases. The plan was to use seven Sopwith Camel aircraft, each carrying two fifty pound bombs, to be launched from the converted battlecruiser HMS Furious and to attack the Tondern base (now in Denmark but then in Germany) on the Jutland peninsula. Tondern was chosen as its Zeppelins kept a close watch on the activities of the Grand Fleet in the northern approaches of the German Bight. On July 17 HMS Furious, supported by the 1st Division of the Battle Fleet and the 7th Light Cruiser Squadron and destroyers left Rosyth and set sail for the Danish coast. Next morning, the Camels were ready to launch from a deck installed in front of Furious's bridge, which acted as a flight deck for the rudimentary aircraft carrier. After a delay of twenty-four hours due to thunderstorms, which also grounded any enemy aircraft or airships that might have revealed their presence, the Camels took off as dawn was breaking and set a course for their target. Almost immediately one of the aircraft experienced engine problems and had to return to Furious. Being unable to land on the ship, the plane ditched nearby into the sea, the pilot being rescued. Taking off from the narrow pitching flight deck in what were demanding aircraft to fly for even the most experienced pilot would have been extremely challenging. Landing was even more so, due in part to the effect of air turbulence caused by the ship's superstructure and funnel.

The Camels reached their target just after dawn, catching the Germans unawares. They attacked in two waves of three aircraft, ten minutes apart, the primary target being the large double hanger that housed Zeppelins L54 and L60. From one hundred feet above the shed the first wave successfully landed three of their fifty-pound bombs on the target causing the two hydrogen filled airships to catch fire immediately, destroying them in a matter of minutes. Moments later the second wave of Camels dived in from the East. The pilots, seeing that the primary target had been destroyed, dropped their bombs on the smaller shed which contained the station's captive observation balloon. Two of the bombs went through the roof of the shed, setting fire to the balloon, and four others fell close to the target but failed to explode. The Tondern base was only defended from air attack by small arms, which caused no damage to the Camels other than a wheel being shot off from one of the aircraft in the second wave. Only two of the Camels, piloted by Captains W. F. Dickson and B. A. Smart, managed to return to Furious, but were unable to land on the carrier and ditched into the sea. Once again, both pilots were rescued. Of the remaining four pilots, three were low on fuel and landed safely in neutral Denmark, where they were interned. The fourth was presumed to have crashed into the sea, neither his body nor the aircraft having ever been found. For the British, the raid, the first ever carrier-launched attack on a land target, was considered a great success, with two of the latest Zeppelins destroyed for the loss of only a single pilot killed.

Undaunted by this latest setback, Strasser ordered what would prove to be the Airship Division's final raid on England, on Monday 5 August, 1918. Five Zeppelins were to take part, including the newest ship L70 with Strasser on board. L70 had flown for the first time only five weeks earlier. Powered by seven Maybach engines and with a maximum speed of 81 mph and a ceiling of 21,000 feet, the L70 class represented the pinnacle of German wartime airship development. Given her speed and ceiling, Strasser was confident of their chances of evading the British defences. During the early afternoon, one by one, the bomb laden giants gently lifted off from their airfields along the North Sea coasts; L53, L65 and L70 from Nordholz, L63 from Ahlhorn and L56 from Wittmundhaven. The three Nordholz Zeppelins flew together at around 16,000 feet, above a layer of low-lying cloud that blanketed the North Sea below. As it was still daylight, the airships, in a loose V formation, waited sixty miles from the English coast in the hopeful expectation that the coming darkness would hide them from the enemy. What may well have concerned the three commanders was that the outside atmospheric conditions of a relatively high air temperature combined with a low air pressure prevented their airships from attaining the desired ceiling. Despite dropping ballast, and in the case of L65 also releasing 1000Kg of unfused bombs, the Zeppelins were unable to climb to an altitude beyond the reach of defending fighter aircraft. At 21.00 Strasser, aboard L70 sent out a radio message to the commanders of the other Zeppelins, ordering the attack on England to proceed. What Strasser could not have known was that the three airships had already been spotted from the Leman Tail Lightship thirty miles north-east of Happisburgh on the Norfolk coast. The position of the Zeppelins was soon passed to the guns, searchlights and airfields protecting the East coast and within forty minutes of the first sighting the Great Yarmouth air station, the closest to where the airships were expected to cross the coast, had thirteen aeroplanes airborne and in pursuit of the raiders. Ten of the aircraft flew inland in search of the Zeppelins whilst three flew out to sea hoping to catch their prey before landfall. The leading aircraft was a two-seater DH4 piloted by Major Egbert Cadbury with observer Captain Robert Leckie, both of 212 squadron RAF. The Airco DH4 had been designed as a day bomber, but proved to possess a performance that made it more than a match for contemporary enemy fighters. Powered by a 375 hp Rolls Royce Eagle engine producing a top speed of 143 mph at sea level, and only marginally slower at its ceiling of 22,000 feet, the aircraft presented a formidable adversary for any Zeppelin. The DH4's outstanding capabilities, combined with its fearsome armament of a forward firing Vickers machine gun and observer's Lewis machine gun, made it the ideal Zeppelin hunter. Both Cadbury and Leckie had already played a part in the destruction of a Zeppelin, Cadbury having attacked L21 in November 1917, while Leckie piloted the flying boat that shot down L22 in May of the same year.

The three aircraft climbed steadily, the DH4 of Cadbury and Leckie leading, with two, less powerful DH 9s following. The DH9s were crewed by Captain C.S. Iron and Sergeant Willis, and Captain B.S. Jardine and Lieutenant E.R. Munday. After forty minutes of climbing through the layers of cloud, the three Zeppelins came in sight. The time was 21.45 and although the sun had set at ground level, at 17,000 feet the Zeppelins stood out clearly in the last glimmers of light from the setting sun. Cadbury and Leckie were at this point two thousand feet below the leading Zeppelin L70, and it took them another twenty-five minutes to coax their aircraft up a further fourteen hundred feet, bringing the giant airship within range. Attacking head on and slightly to port, Leckie aimed his Lewis machine gun at the bow of the L70 and opened fire. The hail of Pomeroy explosive bullets was seen to blow a hole in the airship's outer covering and within seconds flames appeared. The fire quickly spread along the whole length of the Zeppelin and she plunged seawards, stern first. Cadbury estimated that it took barely forty-five seconds for the mighty airship to be completely consumed. The wreckage landed close to the schooner Amethyst, leaving a slick of petrol which burned on the water for many minutes. The Amethyst's crew scanned the surrounding water for survivors, but to no avail. Peter Strasser and the entire crew of L70 had all perished.

With L70 destroyed, Cadbury turned his attention to the next nearest Zeppelin, L65. Seeing the fate of their leader and aware that it would have been suicidal to proceed on their current course, the commanders of L65 and L53 turned away from the pursuing aircraft, hoping to hide in the gathering darkness. Cadbury managed to close to within five hundred feet of L65, allowing Leckie to fire a few rounds before his gun jammed. By the time the jam was cleared the L65 was lost in the darkness. Leckie's shooting had been on target though, his rounds puncturing five of L65's gas cells. L53 and L65 had been most fortunate to avoid the same fate as L70. However, L53's good fortune was only to last another five days. On August 11 she was intercepted over the German Bight by a Sopwith Camel flown by Lt S D Culley. Culley had taken off from a lighter towed at speed into the wind by a Royal Navy destroyer, giving the Camel just enough lift to rise from the short, rolling flight deck. Despite the Zeppelin flying at an altitude close to the Camel's ceiling of 19,000 feet, Culley managed to open fire from around 300 feet below, attacking head on. Using the Lewis gun mounted on the top wing, Culley emptied a double drum of incendiary and explosive ammunition. As Culley passed underneath his quarry, looking back he saw patches of flame along the airship's underbelly which within a few seconds merged into a mighty conflagration. The bow of the doomed Zeppelin pitched downwards and the flaming skeleton descended vertically, bombs and gondolas breaking free as she fell. Once again there were no survivors.

Two days after the destruction of L70 the Royal Navy located the wreckage among sand banks off the Lincolnshire coast at just eight fathoms depth. Over the next three weeks a small fleet of Royal Navy Trawlers brought much of the wreckage to the surface, together with a wealth of technical information and operating records. Some bodies including that of Strasser were found among the wreckage, others were washed up on Lincolnshire beaches over the following days. All were subsequently buried at sea.

The loss of their inspirational leader Peter Strasser, combined with the destruction of two modern Zeppelins within six days, effectively brought to a close the Imperial German Navy Airship Division's strategic bombing campaign against Great Britain. Under the leadership of Strasser's successor, Korvettenkapitan Paul Werther, further operational flights were restricted to scouting missions over the North Sea in support of the High Seas Fleet. Wary of further losses, Werther only rarely deployed the remaining Zeppelins, with much of the reconnaissance requirements being fulfilled by seaplanes. On October 12 L63 and L65 were sent out over the North Sea to provide reconnaissance for a sortie by four battleships and minesweepers, but both had to abort their mission due to a solid overcast of cloud. As they landed back at their bases, the crews could not have known that they would have the distinction of having taken part in the final combat sorties by rigid airships.

Chapter 2

With defeat looming, Admiral Scheer gave orders for a final fleet operation, with the intention of bringing the British Grand Fleet to battle. Cruisers and destroyers, protected by battleships of the High Seas Fleet, were to raid shipping in the Thames Estuary and off the Flanders coast. The losses that the High Seas Fleet expected to inflict would, it was hoped, lead to more favourable terms being offered in the impending armistice. Airship reconnaissance would have been provided had weather conditions allowed. A second titanic battle with the Grand Fleet never took place, sparing the lives of countless sailors on both sides. Mutiny broke out among the sailors at Wilhemshaven and Kiel, with the ships' crews refusing to set sail. As the mutiny spread the Imperial Government lost authority, as Soldiers' and Sailors' Councils wrested control. However, the flight crews of the Naval Airships Division, with only a few exceptions, remained loyal to the Kaiser until his abdication. Nevertheless, insubordination among the ground crews was rife, and in response to a directive from the Fleet's Sailors' Council the ground crews' leaders took control of all the airship bases. No blood was shed, although some officers were arrested but only held captive for a few days before being sent home. Just two days before the Armistice was signed the airships were hung up in their sheds and their hydrogen filled cells emptied. In the febrile atmosphere following the Armistice looting was rife. Stocks of gasoline, spare parts, ancillary equipment and stores were all pilfered. The Sailors' Soviet leaders often turned a blind eye or were complicit in the theft, some making fortunes selling their contraband to buyers in Sweden.

As the months went by, and with the ultimate fate of the Navy's warships and airships still uncertain, a number of flight crew still loyal to the former regime hatched a plot to prevent their beloved airships falling into the hands of the victorious powers. The scuttling of the impounded ships of the High Seas Fleet at Scapa Flow on June 21 1919 spurred them into action. Four days later the conspirators at both Nordholz and Wittmundhaven stealthily crept into the sheds, pulled away the supports beneath the hulls and released the suspension cables, allowing the forty-ton airships to crash to the floor. Devoid of their buoyancy, the airships were under their own weight, breaking the keel and buckling the delicate duralumin framework beyond all possible repair. This was the fate of all the Nordholz airships: L14, L41, L42, L63 and L65, and at Wittmundhaven L52 and L56. At Ahlhorn L64 and L71 were spared a similar fate due to the plot being discovered by the Sailors' Soviet.

The news of the destruction of the Zeppelins brought the rapid seizure of all remaining frontline airships, namely L61, L64 and L71 together with the obsolete L30, L37, LZ 113 and LZ120. The recently completed L72 escaped being seized, albeit only temporarily on the grounds that she was still a possession of the Zeppelin company, having not yet been commissioned into naval service. By the autumn of 1920 the last of the German airships were delivered to the Allied powers. France received L72, LZ 113 and the commercial Zeppelin Nordstern. Britain gained L71 and L64. Italy was awarded L61, LZ 120 and the passenger airship Bodensee. L30 and L37, which were awarded to Belgium and Japan respectively, were both broken up due to the lack of infrastructure to house and maintain the giant craft.

In addition to seizing the Zeppelins, the allies were determined to completely abolish the German airship industry by demolishing the Zeppelin manufacturing facilities at Friedrichshafen. However, the United States, demanding compensation for the loss of the sabotaged Zeppelins which they had expected to receive, successfully negotiated approval for the construction at Friedrichshafen of a dirigible of the L70 type, which became the United States Navy ship Los Angeles. Her construction effectively saved the Zeppelin company from extinction. During the 1920s and 1930s the company continued to build dirigibles, culminating in the highly successful Graf Zeppelin and the ill-fated Hindenburg. The Second World War brought to an end the era of giant dirigible airships, although the Zeppelin company is still in existence, both building and flying non rigid airships, now helium filled, on tourist flights over Friedrichshafen and Lake Constance.

So what did the Strategic bombing campaign achieve? During the fifty-one raids, around two hundred tons of bombs were dropped, killing 557 people and injuring 1,358. Total damage caused was worth around £1.5 million pounds, of which approximately £850,000 was in London. This figure is dwarfed by the production costs of the Zeppelin airships and their bases with their huge revolving hangers. The Nordholz hanger alone, which housed the L33, cost around £350,000 and the L33 herself was built at a cost of over £100,000. Arguably a greater contribution towards the German war effort than the material damage inflicted, came from Britain diverting men and equipment from the Western Front to defend against the Zeppelin threat. The psychological effect on the British public proved to be far less than the German High Command had predicted and public morale grew once airship losses began to mount, beginning with Lt William Leefe Robinson's very visible flaming victory in April 1916 and soon followed in September with the destruction of both L33 and L32 in a single night. Britain was no longer at the mercy of 'The Baby Killers.' The hunters had become the hunted.

Despite the mounting losses in airships and crews the German Navy persisted with bombing raids until almost the end of the war. The Zeppelin crews courageously battled against both the enemy and the elements, aware that with each successive mission the likelihood of death by immolation or drowning increased. Of the fifty or so airship crews trained during the war, around 40% lost their lives.

Despite the increasing ineffectiveness of the airship bombers compared to the Gotha aircraft that raided London from June 1917, money and resources continued to be poured into airship development. A new type of Zeppelin with a ceiling of over 26,000 feet, a bomb load of over 2 ½ tonnes, a top speed approaching 80 mph and a formidable defensive armament of fourteen 20 mm cannons was proposed, but as hostilities drew to a close that leviathan never got beyond the drawing board. The era of the giant airship bomber was over.

Geoff Wass, the nephew of Majorie Costello, ne Hyam holding a piece of the L33, possibly 'liberated' from the wreckage by Marjorie's father, Special Constable Clem Hyam

A Zeppelin for the 21st Century
A tourist flight from Friedrichshafen

Key:

Incendiary: ✦   high explosive: 💥   bomb which failed to explode: ✸   Approximate route taken by L33: ○○○

Bibliography

Books

Brooks, Peter W *Zeppelin: Rigid Airships 1893-1940* (Putnam 1992)

Castle, Ian *London 1914-17 The Zeppelin Menace 1914-1917* (Osprey 2008)

Dudley, Ernest *Monsters of the Purple Twilight* (George G Harrap 1960)

Ridley-Kitts, Daniel George *Military, Naval and Civil Airships since 1783* (The History Press 2012)

Rimell, R L *Zeppelin Volume 2* (Ray Rimell 2008)

Robinson, Douglas H *The Zeppelin in Combat* (Schiffer Publishing 1994)

Stevens, Mary R *"Old Spiery" Mersea's Fighting Parson* (Mersea Island Museum Trust 1983)

Storey, Neil R. *Zeppelin Blitz* (The History Press 2015)

Newspapers

The Daily Mirror 25/9/16

Essex County Chronicle 29/9/16, 6/10/16, 8/12/16

Hull Daily Mail 7/9/17

The Illustrated Police News 28/9/16

The Newsman 30/9/16, 25/11/16

Pall Mall Gazette 25/9/16

The Westminster Gazette 25/9/16, 19/10/16

Public Record Office Sources

AIR 1/613/16/15/307: Information obtained from prisoner of war crew of Zeppelins L33 and L48.

AIR 11/239: Admiralty and Air Ministry: Naval Aircraft Works, Later Royal Airship Works, Cardington: Correspondence and Papers. AIRSHIPS: Photographs. Wrecked German Zeppelin L.33: various components.

DSIR 23/893: Department of Scientific and Industrial Research: Aeronautical Research Council: Reports and Papers. Zeppelin airship L.33: further notes on materials from wreckage

AIR 2/123: Air Ministry and Ministry of Defence: Registered Files. AIRSHIPS: ALL TYPES (CODE A, 6/1): Examination of Crew of Zeppelin L. 33.

AIR 1/633/17/122/89: Air Ministry: Air Historical Branch: Papers (Series I). Admiralty. Report of Zeppelin raid on London.

AIR 10-864: Detailed drawings of L33

CB 1265: German Rigid Airships

CB 1265A: German Airship Plans

www.ingramcontent.com/pod-product-compliance
Lightning Source LLC
Chambersburg PA
CBHW051318110526
44590CB00031B/4390